CHAKORI

~

A Novel

Chandrasekhar Kambar

Translated from the Kannada by
O.L. Nagabhushana Swamy
and
Pranava Manjari

With an introduction by
H.S. Shiva Prakash

PENGUIN BOOKS

Penguin Books India (P) Ltd., 11 Community Centre, Panchsheel Park, New Delhi 110 017, India
Penguin Books Ltd., 27 Wrights Lane, London W8 5TZ, UK
Penguin Putnam Inc., 375 Hudson Street, New York, NY 10014, USA
Penguin Books Australia Ltd., Ringwood, Victoria, Australia
Penguin Books Canada Ltd., 10 Alcorn Avenue, Suite 300, Toronto, Ontario M4V 3B2, Canada
Penguin Books (NZ) Ltd., 182-190 Wairau Road, Auckland 10, New Zealand

First published in Kannada by Akshara Prakashana 1996
First published in English by Penguin Books India 1999

10 9 8 7 6 5 4 3 2 1

Typeset in Palatino by Digital Technologies and Printing Solutions, New Delhi

Printed at Chaman Offset Printers, New Delhi

CONTENTS

AUTHOR'S NOTE

When I was a child, my father used to tell me a story which never seemed to end. It was the story of Chakori, the Yakshi. The story has grown within me over fifty years, and this novel is its result.

Chakori is also the tale of an artist's search for excellence in his art. As I developed my friendship with Pt. Rajiv Taranath I began to marvel at his quest for perfection in classical music. In the process, the tale that I had listened to in my childhood acquired a new meaning. This is what has given my novel its present shape. I do hope that readers will find in it the reflection of their own stories.

Chakori, I feel, is an epic narrative, but not an epic in the mode of Milton or Virgil. The epic is a form of performance which is still alive and thriving among the uneducated people of Karnataka. *Manteswami* and *Male Maadeswara* are two epic performances one can see, hear and respond to even today. *Chakori* has drawn inspiration from the structure of these narratives.

I am grateful to Sri Jayakumar G., an important contemporary artist, for responding to my work with a painting of his own. This painting has been used on the cover of the book.

Bangalore
August 1999

INTRODUCTION

I see it as a privilege to be writing the introduction to Kambar's new novel *Chakori*. I am also aware of the grave responsibility involved in writing about this work which conceals within it the rare ability to linger long in the reader's mind.

Chakori is not just an ambitious work. Even against the backdrop of the entire creative tradition in Kannada, it stands out as a significant experiment. Although the novel shows some influences of *Male Maadeshwara Kavya, Jaanapada Basavapurana, Manteswami Kavya* and other folk epics, its narrative and linguistic richness is unique. It is a refreshingly fresh brew prepared from several ingredients: Akkamahadevi's passionate intensity, Allama's mystical glow, the profound simplicity of Sarvagna's triplets and the lyrical sweetness of Kannada folk songs. The language of *Chakori,* according to me, unfolds a wonder different from the previous wonders of the Kannada language. This is because Kambar has endowed this multilayered work, which is replete with philosophical connotations, with remarkable simplicity. With *Chakori,* he has set an example for the poets of today by demonstrating that it is not necessary always to express thematic complexities in a complex manner.

I am aware that even for a natural poet like Kambar, the mysterious beauty of the language of *Chakori* must have been achieved after much toil. He worked for decades to give an epic shape to the fascinating story of Chakori that had been haunting him since childhood. The rigorous effort of the venture has not been forced upon the reader through the language. Instead, the language of *Chakori* echoes the innocence and sweetness of the sound and the rhythm of the hero Chandamutta's song that brings down the joy of rain from the skies.

I am in two minds about whether *Chakori* should be called an epic or a novel in verse. I feel a little embarrassed to call it an epic. With the exception of Kuvempu's *Ramayana Darshanam*, all other Kannada epics of this century (those written and published before *Chakori*) are epics by right of their voluminous size. Also, *Chakori* is invested with a natural beauty and has none of the solemnity of *Ramayana Darshanam*. Since I am not given to the academic stubbornness of needing to categorize each and every work into a particular genre, I would like not to classify *Chakori* at all. The effortless sense of beauty of Akkamahadevi's vachanas appears to sprawl over the vast stretches of Kannada folk epics. Although the language of *Chakori* draws on different Kannada literary genres, particularly folk and vachana, the path it traverses is all its own. Further, *Chakori* is a departure from Kambar's earlier works, from *Helathena Kela* to *Sirisampigé.* Some germs of *Chakori* could be found in some poems from Kambar's earlier collection called *Belli Meenu*. *Helathena Kela* is no doubt a work of incredible creative power, but one is left wondering if its imaginative richness is a cover for its lack of clarity. Eventually Kambar learnt the art of restraining the onrush of creativity which has born fruit in *Chakori*. There is no conscious struggle here to control the flow of words. The language moves at will to flow, to circle around, move up and down, hide or gush forth in unpredictable ways. A significant achievement of the work is that the natural ease of expression is never given up. Every page bears ample testimony to the beauty and richness of the Kannada idiom. Any reader can collect these gems and string them into a necklace of his or her liking.

Before I read *Chakori*, I had always had reservations about Kambar's writing. Kambar's preoccupation with the past and his indifference to things present were a matter of grave concern to me. For a writer who towered above the rest of our generation, Kambar seemed to force certain intellectual dilemmas into his works. The contrasts between the object and the image, or between fertility and barrenness, I suspected, were being purposely accommodated in his works. *Chakori*, however, has laid to rest all apprehensions that readers like me have had about Kambar. By no means does *Chakori* celebrate the decadent values of the past. On the contrary, it advocates the resurrection of that pure and innocent devotion that is pro-worldly and is concealed in the depths of our collective unconscious.

Chandamutta, the hero of *Chakori*, gathers into a nutshell all the agonies of the world and swallows his sorrows, only to shower his healing moonlight on the living as well as the non-living. He does this through the realization of the primordial melodies and rhythms to which he gives a living form for the sake of others in a fatherless world. The fatherless world is the land of the moon, not the kingdom of the sun. Kambar's works have always been inhabitants of the world of lunar values pervaded by a translucence that does not lay bare mysteries or pull open the secrets of buds. They have always rejected the solar values that drag everything forcibly into light. The ruling deity of Kambar's world, therefore, is Shiva, the moon-decked Lord, and not the sun, which dispels the hordes of darkness.

Transcendental power is conferred on Chandamutta's passion for music by the Yakshi—a being that belongs neither to this world nor the next. Captivated by her, Chandamutta is compelled to free himself from the love of his mother. If a lesser poet were to dramatize the innocent devotions of Chandamutta, the result would have been somewhat ludicrous. To defend radical innocence is the most difficult task for any present-day poet. There are two other characters in *Chakori* who become antagonistic to Chandamutta's love for the Yakshi, a love that wipes out the borderline between the human and the divine worlds. These two are the villains of the piece. The first of the two is Suryamutta, named after the sun. To his credit, Kambar does not artificially prolong the conflict between lunar and solar values personified by Chandamutta and Suryamutta respectively. Soon, a greater villain—Mahaanubhaava—is introduced. This is the character who throws a challenge to the sacred love between Chandamutta and the Yakshi. He too has performed severe austerities to attain the wisdom of music which only the Yakshi can bless him with. However, all his austerities are not free from jealousy and selfishness. He is therefore unfit for the Yakshi's all-giving love. Only Chandamutta, with his selfless longing, is qualified to win her love. This is what paves the way to the ultimate tragedy of the novel.

The contrast between solar and lunar values pervades the whole work. However, it is interesting that the depiction of the contrast is not in black and white. It is not depicted through oversimplified personifications of power and humility either. Instead, the point is made in a very subtle manner. Consider for instance the contrast between Chandamutta's mother and the Yakshi. It is through the broken horn of Punyakoti, another form of his mother, that Chandamutta's music flows out. In other words, Chandamutta can unite with the music-bodied Yakshi only after breaking free from the possessive influence of his mother. Such possessiveness, incidentally, is also a solar value. At the same time Mahaanubhaava, another representative of solar values, also craves like Chandamutta for music, the ultimate value of the lunar world. In short, the oppositions and contrasts that *Chakori* depicts are too subtle to be summed up by mechanical contrasts such as the solar versus the lunar, the masculine versus the feminine, or the scientific versus the artistic. The conflict between terms of opposition appears to go much deeper.

Wole Soyinka argues in one of his critical essays that two mutually opposed but equally tyrannical forces are always at work in history. The first is the dictatorial political impulse intending to control all through the exercise of manipulative power. The second is the all-appealing power of music which also tyrannizes through the exercise of love. What puts up obstacles in Chandamutta's path is the possessive and manipulative thrust of Mahaanubhaava. Similarly, what pulls him down from ecstatic union with the Yakshi is the possessive love of his human mother. Thus, both Mahaanubhaava and the mother represent dictatorial impulses which are opposed to the self-dissolving love of music personified by Chandamutta. The likes of Chandamutta are a rarity in our time and place, as we inhabit battlegrounds of myriad forms of possessive greed. Yet, Kambar has made such a character central to his work. To avoid sentimentality he has made into storytellers dreams hidden in the wakeful sleep of our solar world. Dreams becoming narrators is no doubt a technical novelty. But, in the case of *Chakori*, it is more than that. For dreams are the only region where we, the dwellers of the solar world, can hope to meet out original innocence.

Chakori does not pretend to address contemporary issues. Nevertheless, it seems to me to fulfil a very contemporary need. It attempts to conquer through music, the art of unforced persuasion, the language of tyrannical force which is a chief expression of solar power. This theme is not explored by the novel in the imagined utopias of the past or the future but only in the perennial and ever-present possibilities of dreams. It shows that human suffering is not inflicted on us by defects of systems, but is born with us. Moreover, suffering stems from Shiva, the Primordial Being. If *Chakori* had stopped after merely making this point, it would still be a well-written modernist novel. But it goes deeper: the hero demonstrates through his life and death that it is possible for us to experience and live the oneness of all things through music even while participating in the unending dilemmas of the human condition. The whole of *Chakori* is permeated by a feeling of humility bordering on devotion. At the same time, it is not the world-negating devotion of bhakti poets. This is akin more to the world-embracing devotion of our folk and tribal traditions.

There is a great deal more in *Chakori* that needs detailed investigation. Its unusual narrative skill and unobtrusive symbolism; the characterization of archetypal tendencies that goes beyond the purely allegorical; the aesthetic transformation of the essence of marginalized cultures; the masterful blending of prose and poetry; the polyphonic harmony of wide-ranging idioms and styles—these need separate analyses.

I would like to conclude with an observation about Kambar's mythical mode. Like his favourite poet, W.B. Yeats, Kambar has created a mythical background for his narrative. William Blake, Yeats's poetic predecessor, had done the same. However, there is a significant difference between their mythical mode and Kambar's. The two British poets had to forge their private myths by borrowing from diverse traditions as they lived in a society whose collective myths were crumbling. There is bound to be something synthetic and artificial about the construction of such private myths. The details of Kambar's mythical mode, however, stem from the living myths of a living community of north Karnataka. His mythical mode is comparable to that of Wole Soyinka, who maps out the co-ordinates of present-day experience on the living memory of members of the Yoruba tribe in a way that challenges the grand Eurocentric myths. Kambar weaves a colourful tapestry with strands of a living regional myth. This tapestry has little to do with the selective self-image of the whole of our culture based on, say, the Ramayana and the Mahabharata. Like his great ancestors in medieval Kannada narrative poetry, Kambar writes with no mainstream memories in his bones. At the same time, he has raised this tradition to new poetic heights. It is for this reason that the cultural significance of *Chakori* is no less than its artistic achievement.

I am sure that this many-layered work will continue

to interest readers and inspire writers for a long time to come.

New Delhi H. S. Shiva Prakash

1

PRAYER

Om. We invoke the Shivalinga of Savalgi
Who is the basis of Origin
And pleading with Him, the Lord who is the Sound incarnate,
To show us Truth, we begin our story.

We are the Dreams,
We belong to all times and all spaces
Are of all ages and all minds;
We are the Dreams alive from primordial times.
Gathered together,
On the evening of Maha Shivaratri,
In the yard of the Yakshi temple,
And in the Great,Darkness of the new moon,
Dark as the locks of Lord Shiva of Savalgi,
We narrate the story of Chandamutta, the great artist,
And Lord Shiva himself listens as we tell this tale
Which will keep us awake the whole night;
Those of you who have faith and devotion,
Come here
And listen.
Salutations to the feet of Chandamutta,
Who has borne on his head

The divine foot of Hampi Virupaksha
Seated on the Eduru Basava,
And the divine Mother Pampamma.
Salutations to the divine feet of
Siddarameswara Swami of Savalgi.
Salutations to the feet of father
Basavanneppa and mother Chennamma
Of the Visvakarma clan.
We now sing the story
In the form of a poem.

Those who have not seen Shiva
Come here and listen to the story of one who has.
The Lord himself has declared:
Those who tell this story
And those who listen to it and
Utter the name of Shiva
A thousand times,
Will be liberated from all their karma
And all their desires will be fulfilled.

A thousand times we have narrated, O Shiva
The story of Chandamutta,
And a thousand times we have listened to it, O Shiva
And we have lived that song a thousand times, O Shiva
Once again we shall narrate it as
A new poem set to new tunes
So that, listening to it,
The generations to come
May prosper.
We sing so that
Lord Shiva of Savalgi himself

Should nod admiringly, 'Quite so';
So that the story may enter deep
Into the hearts of the faithful
And illumine their minds.

O Lord, let our song
Shower like flowers
At your all-giving feet
And on the hearts of the faithful.

2

THUS GOES THE PROLOGUE

During that primordial time, when the world of Shiva was a world of shining light, whole and complete, Lord Shiva was happily engaged in *tapas* and meditation. Having meditated continuously for an eternity, he found himself utterly bored one day. So to amuse himself he looked at his face reflected in the nectar that was held in a small cup tied to his waist. Extremely happy at what he saw and desiring to create another one in the same image, he cut off the left part of his body and called that part Adi Maya and she became his playmate. He soothed the wound of his cut by pouring nectar on it and gave some to Adi Maya too to apply on her wound. But she was unable to hold the cup and dropped it, spilling the nectar. Shiva was angered, and in great fury he told Adi Maya that she had better wait till she was old and wise enough to handle the nectar. He then placed it safely in an inner room of his house. 'Look, Adi Maya,' Shiva said, 'play as you wish, and wherever you wish, but do not ever open the doors of the inner room of Great Darkness.' Warning her thus Shiva went back to his meditation.

As he closed his eyes to meditate, Adi Maya who could not contain her curiosity, opened the door of the inner room. In a moment, the Great Darkness contained in the room rushed out and began to spread all over

Shiva's world of brightness and light. When Shiva learnt of the disaster he wished to retrieve at least a portion of his world from this Darkness. He cut off that portion of Shivaloka that was enveloped in darkness and flung it away. Adi Maya, who was screaming for help in the inner room, found herself falling along with that part of the world submerged in the Great Darkness.

The nether half of the world that was cut off thus was not to be found anywhere. Naming a spark of his third eye as the sun, Shiva commanded him to search for Adi Maya. The sun looked for her everywhere; he would rest when he was tired, only to resume the search all over again. The time he took for the search became the day and the time he rested became the night. In this way the movement of time continued and days, weeks, months, seasons, years and ages went by.

Meanwhile, Adi Maya, who remained in the nether half of the world of Shiva, looked around her. What was there to see? If you looked up you saw the sky and if you looked down you saw yourself. The wound caused by the cut from Shiva still burned. Desiring to become one with Shiva, Adi Maya looked up anxiously and grew restless. Her melancholy knew no bounds. Ages passed and as she did not have the nectar any more, her body collapsed and eventually she died. Then . . .

The swollen parts of Adi Maya's body
Became the hills and mountains,
Her perspiration and tears
Became the brooks, rivers and the drops of rain,
Her breath
Became the winds.
Thus the world of mortals
Was created.

As all this happened
An eternity went by.

~

Adi Maya was reborn as the cow, Punyakoti, on this very earth and gave birth to eighty-four hundred thousand varieties of life starting with an ant and ending with an elephant. It happened thus:

In the beginning there was a forest.
There was a cave in that forest.
In that cave was the calf Punyakoti,
The heroine of our story.

She was sad because she had no child.
She was sad because of the relentless silence of the days and
She was sad because of the sleep that filled the nights.
She was sad because she was bored.
Then, while she slept, she had a dream.

In the blue depth of the skies
A magic silver cup shone bright
And disappeared pouring down
The milk of moonlight.
The mind of Punyakoti was stirred
By the primordial desire for union
And she woke up.

By and by, life in the forest
Became dull;
Her eyes, burning red with desire,

Rained tears,
She looked up
And thought deep down in her mind about
How and when she could get that magic cup.
She sat alone, brooding
And her horns brushed against the walls of the cave.

The scratch marks became the images
Of the trees that bear flowers and fruit,
Of the birds that twitter,
And of the bull that is tall as the hills
Grazing in the green fields of the upper half of
    Shivaloka.
This was her devotion to Shiva and his ways.

By her devotion
The image of the bull
Was filled with the vigour
Of Nandisha of the heavens.
Red sparks rained from the eyes
    of the Jogi Bull,
And he breathed smoke from his swollen nostrils,
Kicked his feet to raise mountains of dust,
Bellowed and waited.
Suddenly he advanced and climbed over
The cow in heat and indulged in sexual sport.
The milk in the silver cup of his trunk
Overflowed and
He disappeared into the skies!

Her body trembling and covered in sweat
The great mother came to herself slowly.
She collected the spilt milk in a pot
And put it safely in a vessel tied

To the ceiling by a rope,
And waited.

As time passed Punyakoti
Became the mother cow,
The mother of the trees and plants and crops
The religion of green flourished because of her.
One after another
She had a hundred and one living creatures
Thus was made a world that was abuzz with the
sounds of creation.

Afterwards, eighty-four hundred thousand forms of life took their birth, but the world became a grinding mill of sorrows as these creatures cried from hunger. Do you know what this Adi Maya then did?

To protect her children she poured her milk and blood, growing weak and wasting away in the process. Her body dried up and she lay limp in a well twelve leagues deep. And there she remained as another ten eternities went by.

In the other world, as Lord Shiva sat in deep meditation, a drop of sweat trickled down his forehead and fell on the earth. And from that drop was created the Mortal Man. After blessing the Mortal Man with the boon to enjoy life on earth, Shiva returned to his meditation, closing his eyes once again. But the Mortal Man soon tired of a life without a companion and prayed till the Great God appeared before him, pleased with his devotion. The Mortal Man, his hands folded, pleaded with Shiva thus:

Listen Father, I have no woman in the house,
I have no cattle in the sheds,

Tell me, how can I live alone?
Shouldn't you grant me some support?

To this request Lord Shiva replied thus:

Man, born of my flesh!
In the underworld called Atala, Vitala and Patala,
The Magic Woman of the Mountains Adi Maya has
taken her birth
And now lives in a molehill.
A Satan Serpent called Purushamriga keeps a watch
on her.
Conquer the serpent, marry Adi Maya
And begin your family life.

Thus blessed, the Mortal Man received from Lord Shiva a fistful of hair plucked from his body which he was to use in the event of trouble. The Lord then disappeared.

Following the Lord's instructions, the Mortal Man came to the rim of the well that took one to the underworld Patala, and entered it in search of the Magic Woman. Suddenly he saw before him the Satan Serpent called Purushamriga! He had eyes which were as bright and dazzling as the sun. There were long strands of hair on his body that looked like thorns. Encircling the molehill palace that was a hundred leagues across, Purushamriga raised his hood, taking in the fresh smell of man. Even before the Mortal Man could say, 'O Lord Shiva, what shall I do?' he found himself on the tongue of Purushamriga. Just as you would play with a betel nut in your palms, Purushamriga played with the Mortal Man on his tongue and was about to push him down his jaws when the Mortal Man remembered the hairs that Shiva had given him. He threw the hairs down, and lo and behold, each hair became a thousand Shivalingams and the unseen bells of the heavens began to chime! Immediately Purushamriga spat out the Mortal Man and began to go nine times around each Lingam in prayerful devotion. Seizing this opportunity, the Mortal Man ran inside the palace of the molehill. He broke open the seven gates and there was the Magic Woman of the Mountains weaving a cloth! The Mortal Man was utterly charmed by her beauty. He conveyed to her the order of Shiva. Hearing this the Magic Woman of the Mountains blushed and turned red as red-hot iron, and gave him a piece of the cloth she was weaving. And then, hurrying, she picked up the two horns—the horns that belonged to her from her previous birth as Punyakoti—and ran to the door of Patala with the Mortal Man.

The Mortal Man let the Magic Woman of the Mountains climb up before him. Then, just as he was trying to climb the wall, throwing his right hand and right leg over it, the Satan Serpent came there and began to pull at his left hand and left leg which were still in the region of the underworld! So, the left half of the Mortal Man was in the grip of Purushamriga, while his right half was in the hands of the Magic Woman of the Mountains! She uttered the name of Lord Shiva and kneeling down, pulled at the Mortal Man, tugging at his right hand and right leg with all her might. Then suddenly, there was a noise—like that of tender wood being torn. She fell back as if a rope she had been pulling at had suddenly given away. Panic-stricken, she saw that the right half of the Mortal Man—his right hand, right leg and the right half of his face—had come off in her hands! He was cut along his spine and was bleeding from head to trunk. Seeing this, the Magic Woman of the Mountains screamed in terror.

The Lord of the world, Shiva, saw all this from above and ordered the Sun God who shone over the world from the blue skies to go and help the Mortal Man. The Sun God came down and poured the dazzling light of his red eyes over the right-halved Mortal Man and look, the incomplete body became whole! The Mortal Man came to life as if waking from sleep and in gratitude, he bowed down to the Sun God, touching the earth with his head. The Sun God gave him his blessings for a life of happiness with the Magic Woman of the Mountains. And then the Sun God set.

However, there was another problem at night. The Satan Serpent was left with the left half of the Mortal Man but could not eat what he had got as the body was cut and incomplete. So he spat this half body out onto the earth. Now Lord Shiva called the Moon God who was hiding behind his tangled hair and ordered him to go and help that half of the Mortal Man which had been spat out. The Moon God poured his moonlight on that amputated half and lo and behold, the Mortal Man came back to life yet again. His task completed, the Moon God went back to his abode in the tangled hair of Shiva after blessing the Mortal Man with a happy life.

There were now two Mortal Men where there was only one before. The one who got his life from the Sun God became the elder brother, the one who got his life from the Moon God became the younger brother. But they had a quarrel—who should possess the Magic Woman of the Mountains? Lord Shiva appeared and said that the Magic Woman of the Mountains belonged to both the brothers and that they should share their possession equally. He then closed the door to the underworld, spreading a black blanket over it. He made the elder brother sit over it facing north, made the younger brother sit facing south, and settled the Magic Woman of the Mountains between them. He handed them the silver staff of authority and blessed them saying:

> Live
> Great among men
> But be humble before God.

So saying, he went away to his world of brightness and light. From this point of time began the routine commerce of daily life in the world. The two brothers built a settlement where there was enough work to do and enough food to eat. They also built a cowshed where they raised cattle and sheep in the name of Punyakoti and had milk, butter and ghee. They founded the clan of cowherds and shepherds.

But the quarrel between the two brothers had not ended. They ignored the commands of Lord Shiva and each one claimed that the Magic Woman of the Mountains belonged only to himself. It thus happened that the Magic Woman of the Mountains was forced to live with the one who claimed her at the moment. She was distraught not knowing 'how to walk in two ways at once', and prayed to Shiva for help. Once again, Lord Shiva descended on the earth. He gave the left horn of Punyakoti to the elder brother and the right horn to the younger brother and settled their dispute. Not only that, the Lord also prepared a written document in which he recorded that the right over the woman during the day belonged to the elder brother while the right over her at night rested with the younger brother; that the lineage of the elder brother would be called the Clan of the Sun and the lineage of the younger brother the Clan of the Moon; that the day has one truth and the night has many truths; that the Magic Woman of the Mountains should spend the day with the elder brother and the night with the younger brother. To make sure that the agreement was honoured by the brothers, Shiva appointed the sun and the moon as the guardians of the agreement. But even this did not settle the dispute. One violated the realm and time of the other. The three of them quarrelled so much that Lord Shiva was irritated and after capping the earth with a lid called the sky he returned to his own world.

Now Lord Shiva was no longer there to listen to their complaints and settle their disputes. If earlier the brothers quarrelled for the Magic Woman of the Mountains, they now began to quarrel in the name of the sun and the moon, who were the gods of the two clans.

Once, in an attempt to frighten the younger brother, the elder brother blew the horn that had come into his possession. It sounded like 'Heem' and even before he could put it down, out of the horn's sound flowed the knowledge of making fire, of making weapons, and of winning wars with weapons. The elder brother had sixty-four kinds of knowledge with him now and was extremely happy. He danced in joy.

Now the younger brother also wanted to blow his horn. He did so and it sounded like 'Om', and even before he could put it down, from the horn's sound came twenty-seven Arts—like music and literature—along with us, the Dreams. But the Sun God and the elder brother didn't like us, the Dreams and the Arts. When we were happy at night in the cool light of the Moon God, the Sun God sent lightning and thunder and the kinds of knowledge which could threaten the Arts. The Arts were frightened and sought unknown places to hide in. The Magic Woman of the Mountains grew anxious and sent the Wind God to bring them back, but the Wind God failed to do so. Then the Moon God was asked to protect the Arts. In order to protect them from the anger of the Sun God, the Moon God decided to acquire for himself the nectar from Lord Shiva for two weeks and then give it to the Arts so that they too could become immortal. The day on which the Moon God lay sated with the nectar was called the full moon day, and the day on which he was emptied of the nectar, having given it to the Arts came to be called the new moon day. Six and three—that is nine—eternities were over now. But the brothers' desire for revenge was far from over. In addition to this desire for revenge was the desire for evil. The brothers tortured and cursed each other, they tried to possess, usurp and steal the silver staff of authority, they committed murders. Thus they lived . . . Here we conclude the prologue, and now sow the seed of the story.

~

At the foot of the hill, is a great settlement called Shivapura where Macha and Sirilakki of the Clan of the Moon lived. They had seven sheds full of cattle and seven sheds full of sheep. They were rich but issueless. So they prayed to Lord Shiva to grant them a child, they built temples for the Bhutas, they offered food and clothes for the poor, yet they had no child to call their own. They then turned to the guru of their clan, who told them that they were childless because of the anger of the Yakshi. So, on a full moon day, they made a mandala in the yard of their house, put a bronze pot in the centre of this mandala, and invoked the Yakshi to grace it. They then tied a heifer on one side of the mandala and offered a fertile hen on the other side, lit a lamp and offered to observe five festivals for the sake of the Yakshi. The Yakshi accepted their offerings and in due course, Sirilakki became pregnant.

The couple offered worship to the Mother Goddess on the hill for Sirilakki's safe delivery. On an auspicious Monday, which was also a full moon day, at an auspicious hour, Sirilakki gave birth to a baby boy. The moment the child was born, the father sounded the bells with onions and dispelled the evils with the rite of cutting the umbilical cord. After three days the couple purified the house, observed sixteen types of purificatory rites ten nights later, and named the baby Chandamutta. They then handed him over to the Goddess Shetvi, the Mother Goddess, so that she could inscribe the child's fate on his forehead.

Days passed by. The child drank milk from his mother's breast and crawled, he ate rice and learnt to sit up. Even as Chandamutta the child grew into a boy, Macha, his father, was killed by the dagger of revenge. Widowed young, Sirilakki could now no longer adorn herself with bangles, or bordered saris, or vermilion on the forehead. She was just Lakkabbe, both father and mother to the child. She taught him the trade of the clan, gave a thread for his waist, anklets for his feet and rings for his ears. When she discovered that Chandamutta had an ear for music, she asked the guru of the clan to teach him to play the flute. Chandamutta soon became a young man ready for marriage, but mischievous like a child, he often went off with his friends to tend the cattle and sheep.

3

THE MARRIAGE OF THE YAKSHI*

It was evening.
Abbe hummed a familiar tune
And pounded the grain.
Then came the winds of magic and the rains of
wonder.
In the tender twilight of the evening
The marriage of the Yakshi took place
And the sun went down in the west.

Abbe stood waiting at the door
Gazing at the forest path
Looking for her son who had not yet returned.
The cattle came and went to their sheds,
The son came too, but
Not saying even a word to his mother,
Not leading the cows to their shed,
Removed his footwear, threw away
To a corner the blanket on his shoulder
And the bag, and the flute and his staff.
He went straight to his cot and threw himself
down.

---

* When rain and sunshine are seen together it is said that a Yakshi is getting married.

Abbe heaved a hot sigh
As if burning coal had been poured into her womb.
'Chandamutta, my child, O Chandamutta,
Take off your soiled clothes and wash yourself, son,'
she said.
The son who usually responded thrice
If he was called once
Did not utter a word today.

He has no father, or even brothers,
Whom shall I ask what has happened to my son?
Abbe thought and prayed to the Goddess of the hills.
The friends of Chandamutta came there
Having sent their cows to their sheds.
'Hey you, Kencha, and Decha
You must know better, please tell me
Why is my son silent? He hasn't talked to me,
He hasn't taken off his soiled clothes,
He seems to be sad and is lying down quietly.
Whatever has happened to him? Who has scolded
him?'

'We too don't know, mother,'
Said the boys. 'We don't know the reason.'
But they told her what had happened.
'Today, just as he does every day, Chandamutta
Played on the flute. It was evening and the music
He played was sheer magic.
With their ears pricked up to listen, eyes dreaming,
Even the cows were enchanted
And they slept quietly
In the cool shade of the trees.
Not just the cattle and us, his friends,

Even the trees and plants
Danced to his tune today.
Later, while the cattle slept
We, the boys, amused ourselves in games and fun.
Well, we wanted to play the game of marriage
And we declared him to be the bridegroom.
But Chandamutta didn't agree.
He tried to escape from us,
And ran away into the woods.

'We searched for him.
There, where the three roads meet
Chandamutta was standing
Under a tender banyan tree,
Staring at an old statue of stone.

'Perhaps some angel of the skies
Drawn by the magic of Chandamutta's flute
Had come down to earth
And stood transfixed,
Now turned to stone
Upon hearing our voices,
So we thought.
She was a little virgin,
Her face was pure and bright,
And she had the look of an expert hunter.
She stood erect and taut like a bow
And though she was a statue of stone
Every part of her seemed alive!

'We agreed that the statue should be the bride
And declared the marriage of Chandamutta.
We made a garland of *amritavalli*

And asked him to put it round the neck of the statue.
He did as told.
Oh, mother! How can we ever describe
The wonder of that moment!
We heard from somewhere
The auspicious music of marriage.
The magic wind touched us with all its strength.
We saw the eyes of the horizon
Flashing with a sudden bright light.
The plants, the trees and the creepers
Opened their eyelids.
And on the floor of the woods
We saw a colourful rangoli
Made of flowers.
The earth was thrilled,
We felt it
As the blades of grass
Kissed our feet.
Birds of many colours,
Unable to contain their enthusiasm
Tittered in joy.
The peacocks danced with pleasure.
That tender young banyan tree
Which had a bright ring of green light around it,
That young shining tree
Which ached with its many pleasures
And immersed the birds
In the luxury of sensuous pleasures,
That tree on which we feasted our eyes,
We wondered what had happened to it now.

'Had some angel
Filling the tree with her joy

Made it sing? We wondered.

'While all this was happening
Our friend Chandamutta
Stood there oblivious to the world around him.'

'What is this you say, children?'

'Yes, mother. He seemed lost.
His eyes looked heavy with dreams.
His cheeks were flushed, his whole body
Showed the thrill of some intoxication.
We gently touched his shoulder, and shook him.

'Then, recovering, he looked at us.
His eyes had the light of the other world in them.
He seemed to have returned unwillingly to earth.
He recognized us. But, for a moment, he was
completely lost.

'Immediately he began to shed tears.
Afraid, we asked him
Why he was treating us like strangers
And whatever had happened to him.'

Chandamutta: Someone called me
Someone entered my heart
Someone moved within my mind in
bliss
And disappeared without appearing.

Friends: Why didn't you let us hear
Whatever you had heard?

Come, you crazy fellow,
Don't shed tears.

Chandamutta: I heard the jingling anklets
But I didn't see the feet.
The angel of the pleasure of sound
Danced like a doll in a dome
of emptiness.

Friends: Talk not like this
Words without the thread of reason.
Why do you stand like this
Feeling anxiety at every word?

'However much we tried
We couldn't find out the secret of his sorrow.
The magic wind came again
And the rains.
We were separated.
Now we are happy that
He is safe in his house.
This is the story, mother.'

The mother's heart
Ached as she listened
To the friends of her son.
Chanting the name of
Shiva the Truthful
She went into the house
To see her son.

4

SHE CAME FROM THE HORIZON

Abbe went to the cot on which her son slept. Her eyes searched for him as her feet groped in the darkness. 'O Chandamutta, my son,' she called out, then—her feet touched the head of her sleeping son. She sat down by his side and touched his forehead with trembling hands. Her son's body was burning with fever. 'Oh, my son!' she cried out and prepared a hot potion for him to drink. Then she took him to the cot and put him to sleep. Was it a ghost or a devil that was troubling her son? She prayed to the Moon God, the God of her clan, and took an oath that she would offer garlands of jasmine and fresh meat to him if her son got well before daybreak.

As Chandamutta slept, we, the Dreams, came out. We, who were hiding behind the green leaves hidden by colourful flowers, or the magic Dreams that play with the moon and the stars in the blue sky, all of us in the vicinity gathered around the eyes of Chandamutta and divided our work amongst ourselves.

You, spread the stars
All over the sky
And make a festival of lights.
You go and bring the moon,
But don't disturb the locks of Lord Shiva's hair
And place him in the blueness of the sky.

You—go and gather the winds from the world of
the moon
And make them blow gently here;
Remember that the winds should bring
Incomparable pleasures with them
And the fragrance of the flowers of the meadows.
Bring the sleeping Chandamutta to the woods.
Bring him gently, and let him see happy sights and
wonders.

Where is the Yakshi? Where is she
Who relates the worlds and
Makes them merge into one?
Let her youth be graced
By the bliss of the other worlds.
Let her lotus feet,
With her anklets tinkling,
Bring her straight to the woods.

Did she come near Chandamutta?
Did their eyes meet? Were their gazes entwined?
Did their happiness bloom?
Did their bodies bathe in the thrill?
If so, then listen to the song of Chandamutta:

'Who lurked here? Who
Has come to our region without my knowing it?
Who came here sporting
And forgot the way back
And made my heart wonder?
She with a slender waist
And face like a lotus,
Has the majesty and presence of the other world.

Her nose is like the champak flower,
Her eyes are the colour of the lotus petal,
And flowers drop from her hair
As she bows with the heaviness of her breasts.

'She stood near me, looking down
There were beads of perspiration on her forehead.
Fragrance of flowers unknown spread everywhere
And she stirred and came to me
From the horizon.
Was she a frightened deer
Or the daughter of a god?
Who could know the truth?

'It was like some new and fresh moon
Descending onto the earth,
It was like a desire fulfilled,
It was like a dream tumbling down
From the peak of pleasure.

'The girl flashed her lashes,
It was like lightning,
Like a fountain shooting up suddenly.'

But by then, Abbe came there to wake her son who had gone to sleep on an empty stomach. She caressed his curly hair so we, the Dreams, hurriedly gave up our designs and grabbing the Yakshi from the closed eyes of Chandamutta, ran away.

Why did you wake me up?
Why did you separate the moon from my eyes?

Chandamutta began to weep. The mother's heart trembled at the severity of her son's tone. 'Wake up my son, were you dreaming?' she asked, touching his shoulder.

'The moon was swimming in the bright moonlight. I had caught him with my eyes but you came and woke me up. He has now descended from my eyes to my heart,' he said, clutching his chest.

Abbe's happiness burned out like an ember. She decided to visit the guru of the clan the very next day. Feeling that she ought to take fresh vows in the name of God, she moved towards the idol of the Moon God located in a small niche in the wall.

5

SHE IS FROM A DIFFERENT REALM

The morning star appeared in the sky. Abbe woke up before cockcrow. Picking up the broom she cleaned the yard. She took out the dung and the waste from the cowshed and threw it out. She brushed her teeth, took a bath in the pond and put on fresh clean clothes. She then lit a ghee lamp for the God of her clan. She did not milk the buffaloes or let the calves drink milk from the cows, but looked anxiously at her son still sleeping on the cot. Praying to God to protect her son, she rushed to the guru of the clan who was considered the Elder of the whole earth.

The guru had finished with all the rituals of the morning. He had spread a black blanket on a three-legged seat and was deep in thought. The previous night he had had a dream. His eyes reflected his worry. Just then, Abbe came there and fell at his feet, seeking his protection.

Abbe: My son, after returning from the woods
Didn't speak to me, or eat, or change his clothes
But has just fallen asleep.

Guru: Relax, my child. Tell me the whole story.

Standing there, hands folded in reverence, Abbe narrated her plight.

Yesterday while playing
The children of the village
Performed a mock-marriage
Of my son with a statue.

Whether it was the magic wind
Or the Yakshi fever
Something that should not have happened
Happened to my son.
He is my son, true.
But is he not your disciple too?
Didn't you teach him holding him by the hand?
Didn't you impart the art of music to him?
Didn't you give him education?

Now should his life be ruined?
We have no one else but you,
For us you are equal to God.
Please protect us . . .

He used to reply thrice
If I called him once. Now
He doesn't even recognize me.
He just came home and slept.
If I wake him up
He moves his hands and feet in the air,
He murmurs broken words.
I don't know if it is some magic or some curse.

She then made a vow:

O Goddess Mother of the hills,
I'll offer milk and rice every Tuesday,
I'll offer you chicken and sheep.
Please let my son be as before.

But the guru sat quietly.

'Oh! Oh! You are not saying anything!' wailed Abbe. The guru understood her anguish. As he turned towards the hills and was about to utter a prayer, a messenger came to the door, tapped the earth with his stick, touched his feet and said, 'Guru.'

'Who are you?' The guru asked.

'The Hegde has sent for you. Wherever you are, and whatever you may be doing, you are to come at once and meet him.'

The guru turned to Abbe and said, 'The Goddess Mother of the hills will look after you. You need not worry. Do not say anything rude to your son. I will come and make Chandamutta speak.' And as Abbe touched his feet he placed his hands on her head and blessed her. He took the vermilion from his bag, smeared some of it on her forehead and blew some of it in the direction of the hills, saying, 'O Goddess Mother of the hills,' and then he set off.

6

SHIVA-SORROW

After she had received the blessings of the guru, Abbe went looking for her son but did not find him on the cot. She searched for him near the well and by the bush. 'O, son! O, Chandamutta,' she called out loud and clear. There was no answer and her heart was filled with anguish as unknown fears plagued her. Feeling as if a knife had been plunged into her womb, she hurried to the hollow in the wall where the picture of the moon—the God of her clan—was drawn in chalk, and touching that picture with her hands and lifting her fingers to her eyes, she offered her salutations. Then she turned towards the hills and praying, 'Please protect me, Mother of the hills,' she slapped her own cheeks. 'If you are angry, who else can protect us?' As she spoke to the Goddess, tears filled her eyes. 'I protected my son from the gods who trouble us, but O Mother of the hills, a new misery has now come upon us,' she said like one who felt all the sorrows of the seven worlds. Unable to quieten her heart, she walked to the forest.

She went to where the boys were tending cows but Chandamutta was not there either. She asked the boys where her son was and they pointed to a young banyan tree. 'Why have you left him alone? Have you quarrelled with him?' she asked the boys. They told her:

Today Chandamutta is not what he was yesterday,
Abbe,

We don't know if he wants to speak or not.
Only if we address him ten times will he answer.
Since morning
He has been sitting quietly
Just looking at the horizon
As if it were a mirror.

Who knows whom he sees in that mirror.
He speaks in gestures,
We don't see what he sees
We can't understand his words.
We look at his eyes
But don't see our images there.
His eyes reflect
Just the horizon.
Sometimes,
As if there is a rainbow
His eyes dazzle in splendour.
He behaves like a miser
Who has seen a treasure
But doesn't want others to discover it.
Knowing that he'll shed tears
If we insist,
We didn't ask him what he saw there.
Neither did he speak.
Listen, there's the sound of his flute.
Don't you worry
We'll look after your cows.

Abbe hurried to her son.

7

MY SON IS GOD SHIVA

Chandamutta was sitting on a rock and playing his flute. The breeze in the pasture was gentle, gentle like a flower, and the song was very pleasant to hear. His eyes were closed, soft sunlight was playing on the curls that fell on the sides of his forehead. A black blanket was slung over his shoulder. He was moving his fingers on the flute as if he was attempting to catch an elusive dream in the net of his music but the dream was not rising to the bait. Shutting his eyes tighter, he once again spread his net and waited for the dream that appeared almost to have been caught but escaped as it melted before his very eyes and played hide and seek with him.

The son was oblivious to his mother's presence although she was standing beside him. That moment, the mother realized that her son had grown up.

Looking at the expanse of his shoulders, my son is
an young elephant, she said.
Looking at the peacock feathers tucked in his hair,
my son is Krishna, she said.
Looking at the plaits playing round his shoulders
like little cobras, my son is god Shiva, she said.
Looking at the loincloth of eighteen folds
And the firm and strong thighs and waist
My son is god Kama, the god of love, she said.

And then fearing that her adoration might harm her
son,
In her mind she performed the ritual of warding off
the evil eye.

Her son playing his flute appeared to be lost. So when she patted his back his reverie was disturbed and he opened his eyes. He saw his mother next to him and exclaimed, 'Abbe!'

Her mind was filled with the happiness of discovering the miracle of her son's beauty on the one hand, and the anxiety caused by the words of the guru on the other. So, without saying anything, she took her son home.

Abbe heated some water drawn from the well. Then taking out a silver pot full of oil, she massaged Chandamutta's hands, head and body with it. She then took a piece of soap and some soapnut and took him to the bath, holding his hands.

She poured a hundred pots of warm water over his head and washed him once with soap and once with soapnut. After this she poured a hundred pots of cold water to cool his body, and with a clean towel she dried his hair. Then she gave him a loincloth of many folds and when he went to change into it she allowed herself a smile of pride which she had been holding back till then. Chandamutta walked to the idol of the God of his clan and offered his prayers, reciting the thousand and eight names of the God.

Abbe spread a plantain leaf and sprinkled it with water. She then served *mudde* and two rice, three kinds of meat, six side dishes and fed her son with her own hands.

Chandamutta wanted to go to the pasture. But Abbe

told him to sit down, and spreading his knotted hair on his back, she began to pick out the lice from his head with a colourful comb. She then asked,

'You didn't speak to me yesterday, and went away to the forest without saying anything this morning too. Why did you do that?'

'There's no reason, mother.'

'But then, why did you run away to the forest?'

'In the night I had a dream, mother.'

'What did you dream? Did you dream of any attractive cow? If so, tell me. Let us buy it.'

'No, mother.'

'Did you dream of a beautiful girl?'

Now Chandamutta looked at her face and said, 'I saw the moon in my dream, mother.'

'Did you see the moon or a girl like the moon? Your song today was very, very melodious. Let's have your song, and may you have your girl.'

She cracked her knuckles against her temples in both affection and anxiety. The son, smiling, put on his headgear made of peacock feathers, slung the black blanket over his shoulder, picked up a little sword with a silver handle and tied it to the left side of his waist and hung the colourful flute to the right of his waist. He then held a club in his hand and put betel leaves, nuts, lime and tobacco in a small bag. After readying himself thus, he went away to the pasture. Abbe's anxious eyes seemed to guard the path her son would walk on.

8

THE BIRTH OF A NEW GOD

Sighting the guru of the clan heading towards his house, the Hegde—who was the master of the settlement—waited. A black blanket with floral designs had been spread on the floor which was decorated with patterns made of *akshate*. The betel leaves and nuts were ready on a plate. The guru of the clan—his hair grey, and a bag hanging from his shoulders—came with halaba. Raising his right hand, he blessed the Hegde who received him with folded hands. The guru then took some vermilion from his bag and put it on the forehead of the Hegde, and blew away the vermilion that remained, muttering, 'Mother of the hills, protect.' Sitting down on the blanket, he took some jaggery and cold water to quench his thirst and once again invoking the Mother of the hills, offered her the same. Then turning to the Hegde, he asked, 'Why did you send for me?'

'I am worried. I had a dream, in fact I have been seeing the same dream for three continuous days. That's why I sent for you.'

'What did you see in your dream? Was it a god? Or was it a demon of vengeance?'

'It was a god I had never seen before. That god said that it had come to the intersection of the three roads and declared that if I built a temple for it and honoured it, it would change even dust to gold. On my failure to do so, it would turn everything to ashes! What shall I do now? I'm one who will walk in the light of your guidance.'

Even as the guru asked, 'Which is this new god?' he remembered a dream that he himself had had.

Yesterday, at that time when ghosts go for a walk
I too had a dream!
The bells rang loud and clear in the sky.
The plants and trees all over the hills
Suddenly blossomed and shed green leaves and
    flowers.
In the dazzling bright light
I saw some goddess
Descend from the sky, without the help of a ladder.
I saw the lights of torches
Where the three roads meet!
Suddenly I woke up,
And I was perspiring!

'Is your dream and mine related?' the guru wondered. The Hegde said:

That you also saw, in your dream, the bright light
Where the three roads meet
Is indeed something special and peculiar.
Why don't we go there and see?

The guru enthusiastically agreed to this.

9

THEY BECAME THE DISCIPLES

The guru of the clan, the Hegde, and the elders of the settlement went into the forest to the point where the three roads met, and began their search. The boys who tended the cows were already there. Not knowing what the elders were looking for, they too walked with them quietly. But there was no trace of any new god. Then the guru remembered what Sirilakki had told him and asked the boys, 'Did you see any statue anywhere here?' Eagerly the boys took the elders to the banyan tree and showed them the stone statue but kept their own secret about the games they had played the other day. The younger Hegde, Chinnamutta, wanted to reveal it, but someone seemed to have told him not to open his mouth, so he did not speak.

In a bush they found the statue of a Yakshi. It was a beautiful idol that had opened its eyes wide, wondering at the marvel of the mortal world. On the right shoulder perched a parrot, while the right hand was raised as if to bestow a blessing. The left hand covered the area of chastity between the thighs. The *amritavalli* creeper that Chandamutta had put around its neck during that game of marriage was still there. The guru of the clan understood everything but he did not discuss that matter with anyone.

The messenger of the tribe informed the whole tribe that one person from every house had to participate in the construction of the temple for the Yakshi. Following this announcement, the next day itself all the stone-workers, earth-workers and at least one member from each house came to the woods to carry out the task set by the Hegde. They cleared the area all around and built a small temple, a shrine for the Yakshi who had come into their midst with love and affection. Then they painted the walls of the temple with lime and colours. On the wall on the right, they drew a picture of the Sun God and on the left wall a picture of the Moon God. Atop the temple they hoisted a flag which had a lotus painted on it. On the full moon day, they invited to the temple all the gods of the region, who came there in their palanquins. There were displays and explosions of fireworks. Pipes and other musical instruments were played, and a procession was taken around with shouts of the glory of the new goddess renting the air.

The guru of the clan began the puja at an auspicious moment on that full moon day. He washed the image of the Yakshi with water drawn from seven different places and mixed with holy vermilion and turmeric powder. A hundred sheep, a hundred chicken and a hundred pots of toddy were offered to the goddess. Twenty lengths of coloured cloth, a hundred lengths of flower garlands, *akshate*, vermilion, and turmeric powder were offered to the goddess on a silver plate, as the guru said:

Ours is the offering of devotion
And yours is the power of truth
Please accept our offerings and bless us.

He touched the earth with his head in reverence and prayed to the goddess to accept the offerings. But the silver plate moved away—as if the goddess did not want to touch the offerings.

When the plate moved away as if it was pushed by a human hand, the guru of the clan remembered the words of Sirilakki and invited Chandamutta to offer the gifts to the goddess. But the Hegde requested the guru of the clan to allow his son Chinnamutta to offer the gifts. Even before the guru could say anything, Chinnamutta took the plate of offerings and put it before the goddess and touched the ground with his hands in reverence. But even now the plate moved away and the faces of Chinnamutta and the Hegde turned black in disgrace. The guru of the clan then gestured to Chandamutta to offer the plate to the goddess.

Chandamutta trembled recalling the events of the day before and invoking his father and mother, all his relatives, the Mother of the hills and the God of the clan he put the plate before the goddess. As the people stood around, their palms joined together over their heads in extreme devotion, the goddess accepted the offerings made by Chandamutta. The villagers danced with joy and praised him as the only one accepted by the goddess. All of them agreed that he was to offer worship to the goddess every day and also that a white blanket, a loincloth of twenty folds, seven measures of betel nuts, seven bundles of betel leaves, and the offerings made by devotees during the festivals, should all belong to Chandamutta by right. They also decided to have a *vrata* in the name of the goddess on every full moon day and every new moon day and resolved to celebrate a three-day festival every year in the name of the goddess. Thus they became the disciples of the new goddess.

10

SONG OF A WILD BIRD

The love that Shivapura's inhabitants felt for Chandamutta, as well as the hatred that Chinnamutta felt for him grew stronger and stronger with the passing of each day. Both Chandamutta and Chinnamutta were given lessons in music, flute playing and moral education by the guru of the clan at his house. But with malice in his mind Chinnamutta lost all his concentration and he was full of perverse thoughts. If the guru taught him one thing Chandamutta, on the other hand, derived ten different meanings and interpretations from each lesson the guru taught. 'Where did you learn all these things?' the guru would ask and Chandamutta would reply, 'At your feet, guru.' And if the guru replied, 'I didn't teach you all these things,' Chandamutta would say, 'Then, you yourself should explain, guru,' and touch his feet. Such was Chandamutta's humility that the guru's heart was filled with joy and wonder.

Whenever he heard the sweet music of Chandamutta's flute, the guru would forget himself, and soon be lost in a trance-like state. All those who were nearby, whether they were sitting or standing, would also forget themselves and become oblivious to everything else around them, feeling as if they were floating in a kingdom of joy. They experienced the harmony and thrills of many realities hitherto unknown to them. When Chandamutta finished playing, the world appeared to them a worthier place to live in than it was before. Now Chandamutta seldom went to graze his cattle, neither did Abbe insist that he go. She had invited her brother who lived in a different settlement to stay with them and look after her cows. Though she was happy that her son was the chosen one of the goddess she was however, anxious too.

Every morning Chandamutta woke up at cockcrow, took a cold bath, and carried offerings of new clothes to the temple. After washing the Yakshi's idol with water mixed with vermilion and placing the buds of *sampigé* to the left of the statue, and the tender *hingara* to its right, he would put the new clothes before it. Then coming out of the shrine, he would close the door behind him and stand waiting with his back turned to the goddess. After a few moments, the door would open by itself and the clothes worn the previous day by the Yakshi, would be thrown out and the idol could be then seen adorned in the fresh clothes. Chandamutta would then offer fresh toddy to the goddess and bow his head to the ground in reverence.

Every day, Chandamutta was witness to strange experiences. When in the company of the goddess, he often felt within him a fountain of ecstasy.

One day, as he was coming out of the temple, he felt the desire to grow a garden for the goddess. So he planted a jasmine creeper and to his amazement it grew big the very next day. On the third day fragrant flowers blossomed, filling the air all around with a gentle fragrance. Seeing this, Chandamutta was both happy and afraid. He immediately gathered some jasmine buds in his blanket, prepared a garland and rushed into the temple. Standing before the idol and staring at the face of the Yakshi, he was astonished.

Magician Yakshi, conjurer Yakshi,
Sorceress Yakshi, crafty Yakshi,
Little Yakshi, pure Yakshi with
Tender hair parted in between!
Yakshi the beautiful, with curly hair
Like the dark night!
Her two eyes feel like
Bright twin lamps of ghee.
Her long nose feels like the
Tender bud of *sampigé*,
Her delicate mouth and lips are
The moonlight which in laughter
Has showered its love.
Look at her image—
Like that of a peacock just about to dance.
Chandamutta, full of appreciation
His whole body seized by the frenzy of love,
Set the garland of jasmine on her head.
Soon the buds crackled and blossomed!
A bud for loveliness! Another one for beauty!
One more for love! Then, when he gently touched,
As if he didn't touch at all,
Her cheeks, his hands felt,
Oh, God!
The hot breath of excitement!
Who could it be?
His whole body felt the flash of lightning
And he took the flute from his waist
And put it to his lips.

Then someone picked the songs of the wild birds

And sprinkled them on the boy and chuckled.
He caught the songs floating in the air
With his flute and played on
And danced to the rhythm of his songs.

The tunes brought the Yakshi to life.
Suddenly liberated from her stoniness
She hurriedly ran her hand over the new clothes.

Using her palm as a mirror she looked at her face,
Gently straightened her curls,
Touched and felt again and again
The garland in her wet hair.
Light shone in her eyes
And she floated in that light
It was a celebration of joy.

Chandamutta, the handsome boy, danced
Oblivious to the thorns or piercing stones,
Chandamutta, the good-looking boy, danced
Not caring for the bushes and pitfalls.
As the song rushed, wave after wave, and carried her away
The Yakshi lost her balance and recovering soon,
Said, 'What an experience this is, O mother!'

She danced like a peacock. But the rough earth and crude stones hurt her tender feet and she cried out in pain.

O boy of haste, O boy of eagerness
Like a flowered sugar cane
Beautiful, greater than anyone,

I, who has never
Stepped on earth,
How can I dance?
But, how can I at the same time, not dance?
Stop, please stop.

Chandamutta did not hear anything of what the Yakshi said.

Hey, look at this boy playing on his flute and dancing
Making every part of my body go mad and crazy
A black blanket on his shoulders, feathers tucked in his headband
He dances like a peacock in the monsoon.

He came thinking I am a stone
Held my long wet hair in his left hand
Put the jasmine garland with his right hand
Straightened my curls, and became a feast for my eyes.

I could not help feeling a thrill
My whole body perspires through every pore
God of the settlement, I cannot live
Half a moment without you.

Stop, shepherd boy, stop. Don't play the flute.
Don't drive me mad with the tunes of your song.
What will people say if I follow you
And what will the other gods say in anger?

Teach me, the women who know
I am no longer a goddess

I am now obliged to his art
And this beautiful boy's innocent love.

Just then some noises were heard. The Yakshi hesitated—only to hide herself in the stone statue once again.

11

THE SWAN COUPLE

While the Yakshi was thus immersed in fear and devotion and the love of Chandamutta, here—

The heart of Chinnamutta was filled with fumes of hatred and he was blinded with jealousy. He heard that some Yakshi of great magical powers had fallen in love with Chandamutta; that every day she changed her soiled clothes and accepted clean clothes brought by Chandamutta; that each day she taught him a new lesson that gave him new powers.

He said ugly things about Chandamutta
And felt great joy.
Cooked up false stories
And exaggerated them as he narrated
The colourful stories in the streets.
As he chanted a thousand times the bad qualities
    of Chandamutta,
That he had made up,
It was time for the first fair of the Yakshi.

We do not like Chinnamutta. We do not like him because he does not like Dreams. But as he has already stepped into the narrative we cannot just leave him out. Thus by telling you about the wonderful incident that we witnessed, we proceed with our narrative.

Chinnamutta, an only son and motherless, was

doted upon by the elder Hegde and lived like a lord in the lap of luxury and wealth. A tall person, his body and mind had been hardened by continuous practice of physical exercise and wrestling. As he exposed his body to the sun for long periods of time, it became hard—like a burnt brick. Arrogance personified, he never joked even with his equals and whether in a ball game or a game of marbles or *chinnikolu* he simply could not stand defeat. He could render a person speechless by simply knotting his eyebrows. And he could not see at all at night. As the people of the Clan of the Sun lacked the ability, patience and discrimination to see the truths of night and darkness, this limitation of Chinnamutta was not surprising.

One day early in the morning by the pond, Chandamutta began playing upon his flute as he had just completed his worship of the Yakshi. The mist moved over the pond like a thin sheet of smoke. Even the sweet-tongued birds stopped chirping and listened to the flute of Chandamutta. A young swan couple, like the dream of the pond, gently glided in the pond, their eyes half closed as they listened enraptured to the flute. We the Dreams stood there, mesmerized and silent, our feet firmly fixed in the glittering green surroundings of cool divine peace. Suddenly we heard the splash of someone jumping into the pond. We were anxious as we did not want anything to disturb the swan couple. Lost in the enchanting music of the flute, the swan couple were happily oblivious to the happenings around.

The person who had jumped into the water was Chinnamutta. When he realized that it was Chandamutta who was playing the flute his happiness left him. His face turned black even though he was in the cool pond. Quickly he finished his bath, put on a new loincloth and tied his hair into a knot. And when he saw the mesmerized swan couple, he felt as if someone had put chilli powder into his eyes.

His eyes burnt like the fire of graveyards.
He boiled in ferocious anger.
He lost his mind and thought evil thoughts.
He picked up a sharp stone
And prowled with silent steps,
Found an appropriate spot
And took aim
And, oh God
Threw the stone at the swan couple!
It broke the neck of the cob
And he could not even shriek,
But beat his wings
And drowned!
The pen did not know a thing
But seeing her mate drown
Screamed out loud.
The birds in the trees screeched
And made unfamiliar ugly sounds,
Squealed and blared
Scratched themselves with their talons
And pierced each other with their wings.
The pen opened her eyes that had
Turned red in fright
And looked at Chinnamutta in anger.
She flew towards him
Like an arrow.
Chinnamutta disappeared in fear.
Our minds and hearts were wounded.

We did not dare look at the sorrow of the pen.
We left Chinnamutta, his madness, his company
And came here, Shiva.

The pen did not fly anymore, neither did she sing, or join the other birds. Neither did she eat or drink. She just stood, waning like the new moon, on the bank of the pond where her lover swan had been murdered. Unable to contain our sorrow, we tried to console her. Pleading with us she asked, 'Will you please bring him here once, just once? I promise you I'll do him no harm.'

We agreed.

That night we made Chinnamutta see the pen in his dream and gave him the message, 'Go to that place where she is.' He woke up suddenly, breaking into a sweat. He wiped it off and went back to sleep, but he did not come to see the pen in the morning.

The next night we showed him the same dream again and once again he was afraid. But still he did not come. Though we made him dream the same dream for four, five days he did not come. Then we showed the same dream several times on a single night—in fact, whenever he closed his eyes. Now he knew that he could never be free from the dream, and on a Monday morning, arming himself with a sharp knife and a spiked club, he came to the pond.

The pen recognized him from a distance and her eyes shone as Chinnamutta stood leaning on his club. The lady swan came walking to him and standing before him, she spoke in the voice of a human.

You took the life of my lover. Didn't you?
Now please take my life too.

As she spoke, she sat upon her hind and tore at her heart with her talons. Oh God! Oh God! Her innocent heart was ripped apart and blood splashed all over Chinnamutta's face. Even before we were aware of what was happening, her neck fell detached from her body and she was dead. A few among us could not bear the sight and screamed aloud, some beat their breasts while some others covered their faces with their hands!

This is what we know about Chinnamutta. Now as we complete this story, it is time for the fair of the Yakshi . . .

12

IT IS THE FAIR, BROTHER

The young and the old of Shivapura, along with their servants and attendants, bathed, dressed in new clothes, lit festive lights in their huts and worshipped the gods of their clans; they decorated their cattle and sheep, the treasures of their lives with flowers and garlands. Then, as the drums and pipes and all kinds of musical instruments played on, they moved under the leadership of the Hegde and the guru of the clan, towards the temple of the Yakshi. Chandamutta, following Abbe's order, took a bath and put on his best loincloth decorated with little pearls and bordered with glittering silk; a silver bracelet adorned his wrist and a silver flute was tucked at his waist. Chinnamutta was dressed in a silk dhotra, and had put on gold jewels; there was a ring of pearls on his finger and on his wrist was a gold bracelet. He also carried a flute with little jingling bells.

The Yakshi temple was cleaned with water mixed with cowdung; a canopy of sugar cane sticks and betel leaves was made and a lamp was lit. The God of the settlement, the God of the hills, and all the other gods of the region were invited to the temple and incense and gifts were placed at their feet.

Chandamutta washed the Yakshi's idol clean, dressed it in fresh new clothes, adorned it with gold and silver ornaments, put vermilion on its head, put *sirisampigé* to the right of the idol and tender *hingara* to the left, and bowed down touching the ground with his head. Then the devotees offered a herd of sheep in sacrifice, burnt more incense and lit lamps. Then, bowing before the idol, they prayed:

> Please give us milking cattle and sheep
> And enough forest to graze them.

By the time the worship came to an end it was almost that time of the evening when the dust from the feet of the cattle returning home fills the air.

Now, one after another, the villagers stepped forward and displayed their arts. The stick players sang a song and danced to the beat of sticks:

> It's the fair, brother, it's the fair
> Of magician Yakshi, it's the fair
> As mango groves blossom and
> As parrots sing, it's the fair.

As they danced with vigour the dust rising up from their feet touched almost the tops of the coconut trees.

Nobody wanted to return to Shivapura just yet. Then an elderly man said, 'Let the disciples of the guru of the clan show us some of what they have learnt.' As if he was waiting for such an invitation, Chinnamutta immediately picked up his flute with the little jingling gold bells and gently began to play a tune. He selected appropriate notes and played them so skilfully that the tunes appeared to be very natural. The villagers were happy to hear his music and after this, they declared that it was now Chandamutta's turn to play his flute.

Chandamutta looked at the feet of the guru who

gestured to him to go ahead. Chandamutta then tied up his hair into a knot and bowed down at the feet of the master. He invoked the truthful Lord Shiva, his own father and grandfather, and brought his silver flute to his lips.

As he selected sweet notes
Mellowed and tempered
And began his music,
The Moon God appeared on the eastern hill
And effortlessly
The magic of the tender moonlight
Spread everywhere.
Here, below,
The creeper of happiness
Spread itself to the horizon
And there, above,
Up to the moon.
As the waves of the song
Filled the air, the transposed people
Exclaimed in silent wonder.

Hearing Chandamutta's flute playing, Chinnamutta was burning with flames of jealousy. Chandamutta noticed this and he was enveloped by a desire for revenge. So he played the same notes that Chinnamutta had played earlier, to show him in poor light.

The sense of challenge grew, defiance grew even stronger
And he played such tunes one after another that he made the people
Appreciate him in a thousand and one ways.

As the rays of the moon became intense, almost
burning,
Chinnamutta paled and became dull.
And Chandamutta got more excited in his
happiness.

He was about to pick up a new tune to play when suddenly, the song stopped as if the thread of music had snapped. The hills appeared to laugh aloud and as the shocked people turned around to see—

There she was standing, behind them, an old
woman,
Old, ugly and dirty.
She laughed out loud, her mouth full of teeth,
And looked at Chandamutta as if to slight him
She stood connecting the sky with the earth!
Nose dirty, eyes red, red hair scattered,
And tucked with stars, neck full of rudrakshi beads,
Blouse torn, sari tattered,
Breasts and ears hanging, and a bamboo instrument
in her hands.
She was in great anger,
Made unusual noises, threw her hands about, and
rolled her eyes.
Her face contorted and hideous
Oozed bad odour that made the people retch in
disgust!

The young and the old slunk back in fear. They felt that the hills, temples and houses had all collapsed. Some thought that she was a demon from some unknown world, and swooned from the fear that they would never return to the safety of their homes. Some sat transfixed, unable to move.

She pointed her stick towards Chandamutta and thundered—who? That ugly and dirty old woman!

> Hey,
> If what this creature has played is music
> What about true music? Is it dead?
> Have truth and justice disappeared?
> Have the rains above dried up
> And the crops below burnt to ashes?

Her crude speech lashed out like waves on those gathered around.

Now, the guru of the clan was the only person who could muster up some courage as the others merely stood in fright holding their breath in anxiety. The guru wiped the beads of sweat from his forehead and with folded hands mumbled, 'Please excuse our thousand and one errors, if only you could say who you are . . .'

Old Jogti: No one has given a name for me. I am, and my truth is. If you have eyes, look. I am not one born of flesh and blood. I am not one to be wet by water. In the pond called the expanse of the sky, and within the three-petalled flower called the white lotus, I was born. I'm the mistress of Time. Who are you, old fellow?

Guru of the clan: I am merely the dust of your feet. I am the guru of the clan. I'm the one who taught these boys the art of music.

She spat on the guru's face and uttered several words of contempt—who? That dirty old woman with burning eyes.

Old Jogti: Thooo . . .! Let fire burn your decrepit
powers!
You, a guru of this worthless music?
Tomorrow, when kaliyuga comes
from the west
Measure out and sell this music of
yours!

Look, look, there sits a monkey,
Look at it.
Oh! Look, look at the light of the
shepherd clan,
Look at it.
Oh! Look, look at the pinnacle of your
settlement's fame,
Look at it.

She pointed to Chandamutta who was by now shivering with fear and ran towards him. That old lady of vengeance clattered her teeth and said:

You worthless fellow, don't be proud of your worth
I know what your true worth is.
Can you play like this?

She then took off her tattered sari and wore the same like a man's dress. Breaking a portion of her chandike she put it to her lips as if it was a flute. When she played, oh God, all the worlds, all the people, eight hundred million creatures, from the ants to the elephants, were immersed in the moonlight music of the flute! They were rendered silent in their wonder! They remembered the aching pleasures of their many, many lives! Her music brought before their eyes the gods who are always invisible with their ethereal bodies! Feeling utterly blessed, the people seemed oblivious to their own bodies when suddenly,the old Jogti stopped playing, ran towards Chandamutta, snatched his flute from his hands, broke it into two and threw it upon his face. And before the people could understand what had happened, she had disappeared into the forest, who? That old Jogti!

13

FROM THERE, THE MOON IS JUST A FEW FEET AWAY

Who has soured the fresh milk?
The moonlight thickened
And enveloped the fields of Shivapura
The disturbed fair came to an end.
The land and the people were intoxicated
By the song of Jogti.
Eyes became heavy with sleep
And the whole settlement was drowned in the sleep
of Maya.

Chinnamutta had been angry with Chandamutta for the latter had played the same songs that he had played and what's more, had played them better. But now that Chinnamutta thought that the old Jogti had taken up his cause and settled the score with Chandamutta, he was extremely happy and could hardly sleep in his excitement.

The guru of the clan too could not sleep, intoxicated as he was by the divine experience.

Chandamutta could not sleep either. He wanted to fall at the feet of the old Jogti and learn music. He decided to see the Jogti at once and reverentially invoked his father, grandfather and Shiva. He then put his blanket on his shoulders, took up his cane and went to seek the blessings of Abbe.

In the yard Abbe was sitting, leaning against a rock.
There was a platter before her
And it was filled with water.
The reflection of the moon played in it.
Chandamutta came silently
And sat beside his mother.
The reflection of the moon
Appeared to talk to her.
And the mother seemed to whisper
Silent complaints to the moon
But Chandamutta could not understand that
language.

Abbe said:

Do you remember, child?
When you were young and tiny,
You nagged and pestered me for the moon
Which reflected, split and became whole again
In the water of the pond.
You were stubborn,
Threw away your necklace and bracelet,
And sat up without having food or water
Or even lying down to sleep.

Me, the mother, frightened and wondering,
Said—'Look child, the moon
Enacts his story for the little fish in the pond.'
Do you know what you did?

You took some water in a platter
And looking at the reflection of the moon

Asked him to tell you his story and cried.
You cried and cried and then went to sleep
    in my lap.
The moon too
Played and played in your curls
And slept.

In the morning
You showed me the jasmine in our backyard
And said,
'Look mother, these jasmines of our house
Mock the day moon.'

Do you remember all that, my child?

Chandamutta, not saying anything, sat there rubbing his face affectionately against his mother's back.

'Today is the full moon day. Isn't it? Come on, drink this,' she held up the platter before her son as it was the practice of the clan to make the children drink water from a platter in which the moon was reflected. This was done in the belief that such water would make the children strong.

'Am I still a child, mother?' Chandamutta said and putting the platter to his lips he drank eagerly. Did he drink the moon or the moonlight! His mind and body were immediately cooled. The competition with Chinnamutta, the appearance of the ugly Jogti, her song, his hunger for music, the loss of his flute, the moonlight he drank, everything was encompassed in the magic of his mother's love. Feeling soothed, he lay down on her lap.

'Mother, mother, please sing that lullaby that you used to sing when I was a little child,' he said. The words of her son were sweet as sugar. Abbe's heart overflowed with affection. She sang:

On the silver hill by the juggernaut of wild flowers
Streams flow full of milk. And if you see,
The moon is just a few feet away from there.

Quick, close the doors, girls, the Yakshi from
The moon world will come. And steal away the child
To the land of fairies.

The sorceress Yakshi will make you see
No one but herself. My child please don't
Open your eyes forgetting this warning.

Chandamutta did not know when he had fallen asleep listening to his mother's song. When he awoke, he found himself on his mother's lap in the yard. The moon was still pouring down his silver light over the world. Perhaps because of the moon-reflected water that his mother had made him drink, he felt a great hunger for light and sat up suddenly. Abbe had gone to sleep leaning against a rock. Chandamutta stood up quietly and touched her feet and sprinkled the dust from her feet over his head. He then picked up his blanket and stick and went in search of old Jogti. Abbe was mumbling:

The Yakshi from the moon world came
Her palms full of moonlight
And sprinkled it,
Showered it,
Tossed it,

Smeared it all over her body,
Ate it, drank it,
Swam in it, flew over it,
Filled it in her eyes and heart,
And put the song to sleep
Over the wet green,
And she too slept.

14

HE MADE A THOROUGH SEARCH

Invoking Shiva Chandamutta began his search that Monday at midnight. Chandamutta remembered Shiva and began his search. He tried to guess the direction in which the Jogti had disappeared, and then followed in the same direction. Looking to his right and to his left, he climbed the hills, wandered in the forests and searched for her. He saw the wild animals and birds, looked intently at the dark shadows created by the moonlight under the rocks and also looked at the tree tops to see if she was hiding there. It was dawn, the Sun God had appeared in the east and the chirping world of birds had awakened. Chandamutta suddenly remembered that he had not performed the Yakshi worship that day. He felt guilty for having let down the guru of the clan, the gods of the settlement, and his mother who was equivalent to mother earth, who had trusted him and had given him the responsibility of the Yakshi worship. Above all, he had been disloyal to the Yakshi. Chandamutta beat his head with his stick and as he sat repenting, a little parrot in flight gently touched his head. It aroused in him the memory of the old Jogti's song and he decided that his life was futile if he failed to learn to sing like her.

'Old woman of music,' he shouted aloud and searched. 'Jogti of songs,' he cried out and searched. He climbed up and down the hills and searched. He roamed the thick forests and dreary fields and searched. Unmindful of his hunger or thirst, without stopping for sleep or rest he searched the eastern hill, the western hill, the southern and northern hills, the hill of tigers and the hill of elephants. He asked everyone who lived in the nearby settlements and huts about the Jogti. He begged the hunters, beggars, sadhus, dasayyas and yogis. He questioned men and those who appeared like men about the Jogti. All of them said:

From the day this forest was created
And from the day we built our hut
We haven't seen one like that.

Chandamutta walked and walked with all kinds of thorns piercing his feet. He stumbled over hard rocks and developed blisters. Then he fell onto the earth and crawled. Unable even to crawl anymore, he lay under the shade of a boulder at the bottom of the hill and slept for a long time. When he woke up he felt refreshed and in an undertone he tried humming the song that the Jogti had sung. But he found to his utter alarm that he could not sing for his voice wouldn't come out. It was as if his vocal cords had been severed. Afraid and grief-stricken that he had lost his song, he searched for his flute on his person and looked everywhere he could. He then remembered that the Jogti had broken his flute. Had she broken his flute or his neck! Annoyed that his song was stolen, he sobbed.

Oh song, who made happy the little boy who played
in the dust
Oh song, who bathed the boy in the gold of sunlight

And in the silver of moonlight as he tended cattle and
sheep
Oh song, who carried the boats of magic from
beyond the horizon
Oh song intoxicating,
Where have you gone?

The song that the winds of Time have carried away
Boy, you'll never find it again.

Gone for once, and gone for ever
How can you learn the same song again?
You must learn to become empty
And learn again to fill
When a new light comes rushing.

But, Shiva,
What burden of knowledge
You have put on these tender shoulders!

Lost in thought, Chandamutta closed his eyes again. When he opened his eyes, what magic, what wonder! She was sitting before him, like a female Shiva, her eyes closed, with little snakes in her hair. Who? That old Jogti!

'Jogti!' Chandamutta cried out loud and leapt as if to catch her. But she had recognized him and was scheming her escape.

Standing at the mouth of the cave,
She gestured to him with her eyes and hands.

Chandamutta rushed to her and stood before her with his hands folded, and requested, 'Please, Jogti, teach me your song.' But she waved her stick and made him stand at a distance.

> You cowherd brat, you shepherd kid,
> What song? And who are you?
> Go away!

She was angry and Chandamutta was incensed too because she was being disrespectful about his clan. Nevertheless he controlled himself and said, 'Didn't you break my flute?'

'Oh, did you come for the flute? Then follow me,' she said and took Chandamutta to the edge of a ravine and asked him to look into it.

'What do you see?'

'A bottomless pit,' he replied, looking down into it.

'That is the world of your forefathers. Your flute is there. Go and get it.' With that, she pushed him down and quietly disappeared. Who? That sorceress, old Jogti!

It was his good fortune that Chandamutta came out alive from this nightmare. He had only lost his consciousness. When he came to, he realized that he was in a mire. All around him was the darkness of illusion. His whole body ached. In that desolation, there was no living creature he could ask for help, let alone a human being. Hoping that someone would come and pull him out of the mire, he moaned out loud. As no one answered his cry, he remembered his mother and wept. Then somehow, we do not know how, he managed to crawl out of the mire by himself.

He saw the Jogti in his mind. His eyes burnt as if some chilli powder had got into them. The impenetrable darkness closed around him. He was angry as he thought about that deceiving old hag.

> O Shiva, how can I tell you
> How the old Jogti has wounded me,
> My life is shattered
> By her harassment.
> She broke my flute and snatched my song.

He boiled in mad fury for a moment and then the memory of her song filled his mind.

> Your song, O old Jogti, like the venom of a snake
> Creeps up all inside my body and mind
> Makes me sleep and die.
> My dream is lost
> And what remains is
> The path of its escape
> And the darkness of lost hope
> And the two eyes that stare at the path.

He wept endlessly.

A long time passed but the darkness still remained. This must be some doggish hell—murky, black, gloomy darkness. Darkness that could be felt. Darkness that enveloped the body. Darkness that had put out even the stars and turned the world to a solid mass of charcoal. Chandamutta remembered the moon—the God of his clan. The moon appeared in his mind, but darkness filled every corner of his mind and reduced the moon to a piece of burnt coal. Desperate Chandamutta closed his eyes and felt the darkness was within him. Nothing remained except that little ego called 'I' and he did not know what to do with that ego. He wanted to surrender it at Shiva's feet.

He groped around with his hands and found a stick which had a sharp edge—as if it was honed. He thought it was sharp enough and pointed it at his stomach. He then remembered his parents, relatives, members of his clan, his companions, the dead old cow Punyakoti, and the calf, the black dog and the white dog. Thinking that his life had finally come to an end, he invoked the God of his clan—the moon—but just as he was about to stab himself, he heard a voice piercing the silence of the impenetrable darkness. 'Wait. Why this hurry?' The voice was accompanied by a tinkling of little bells. He saw two green lights, as if the darkness around him had found a pair of eyes that were now approaching him. As they neared him he felt as if he had got a new pair of eyes. There it was, the miracle of the three worlds—a three-legged creature! Except for its two eyes, everything about that creature seemed to be made of bones. It was an animal or a creature of the other world which had just come out of its grave! Chandamutta's heart pounded madly. The creature had no lips which gave the impression that it was perpetually smiling, and as he listened to it, Chandamutta felt his being renewed with a new lease of life.

'Do you know what it is that you are holding in your hand?' the animal asked. And when Chandamutta looked at his hands he saw that they held a horn of a cow.

'Do you know whose horn that is?'

'I do not, O Sacred Feet of Shiva.'

'That is the horn of your dead cow Punyakoti. Do you need a better flute than that to play the tune of moonlight on, boy?'

And as it uttered these words, the animal vanished into thin air!

Those eyes that were like green diamonds, the forehead that was smeared with sacred ash and sandal, the shape of the animal and what it had said . . . the boy remained wonderstruck and it was a long time before he shook himself awake to return to our world.

The horn was about the length of an arm and without any curves or knots, but straight and beautiful. Chandamutta felt proud that it was the horn of Punyakoti, the cow of his clan.

Chandamutta sharpened the horn smooth
Made a hole for the breath
And turned the horn into a flute.

He made eight more holes in it
So that the Life Breath flowed through the nine holes
And thus Chandamutta made a female flute.
He drew a picture and decorated it with flowers
And requested, 'Mother, please grant me the lost song.'
His mind full of devotion
He put the flute to his lips.
He controlled his breath at his navel
And slowly filled the flute with the breath he had held back
And created the sound of Om.
He gently played a tune
That was like the call of a sad mother deer
For her lost fawn.

Like a fawn that had lost its way in the forest, he saw the song. His heart aflame with this sight, he played the flute again. The young deer quivered as the gentle music of the flute touched it. It crept forward in amazement and wonder. Chandamutta played the flute in a way that reminded the little deer of feeding at the breast of its mother. He stole up behind the fawn and caught it suddenly. The deer calf felt warm and soft. Chandamutta nestled it in his arms, fondled it and smelled it and enjoyed this sense of touch. He felt elated and as he tightly embraced the fawn, he lost his sense of rhythm. The song stopped and the fawn leapt out of his arms and disappeared into the forest.

In this way the song kept on eluding Chandamutta, who would nevertheless pursue it with determination. This game went on for several days. One day as he searched for his song in the forest, he stepped on a creeper covering an abyss, and fell into the chasm of the underworld.

15

WHAT WORLD IS THAT!

Chandamutta who had fallen
Slowly regained consciousness,
Opened his eyes, and
Oh, God! What kind of world was it that he saw!

There was no Sun God above
Or even the moon, the God of his house,
And no one to ask or listen to him.

It was a world of heavy silence
A death-like silence settled
In the womb of the vast expanse!
It was not day, nor was it night,
Green isn't like green, trees aren't like trees.
There's wind that doesn't blow and water that
doesn't flow.
The sky above is a perturbed dream
The curses of the world have assumed different
shapes
And descended on the earth.
Happiness is a heap of ash.
Pleasures are but burnt charcoal.
And in each corner is stockpile of manure
Of the broken pieces of the rainbow.

The world that is too much with us when we open
our eyes
The world that anguishes the heart when the eyes are
closed
Oh God, which is the path that I travelled on
Where is the road that I should take
From where did I come here
What country is this, what world, what hell?
Like a calf separated from the herd
Chandamutta moved restlessly.
Filled with fear
Unable to sit still or stand straight
Unable to decide what to do next
Uncertain whether he was alive or dead
He pinched himself
To make sure.
He shouted the name of God loud and hoarse
But he could not hear his own voice.
He was sure that he was dead.
This is the world
Where the sky and the earth
Have changed places,
This is the world of Yama, the Lord of Death,
He decided
And collapsed to the ground
Desperate and forlorn.

Thank God! By the grace of Shiva Chandamutta could hear someone singing in the distance. It was like the cool wind, the mercy of God, that brings the movement of life to a lifeless world.

Almost near the horizon, atop a hill, there was a Shiva temple with a thousand and eight pillars and the blue sky itself spread like a roof over the pillars. If you entered, you would see at every turn huge pillars supporting and holding up the sky. There was nothing but darkness in the dome of the sanctum. In front of this sanctum lay munching the Bull of Shiva quietly and peacefully. By the side of the sanctum a pot-bellied man sat in exaltation, attempting to tie together the threads of a song. His hair was dishevelled, like the fronds of a palm tree in the wind, his eyes were red hot balls of iron, his head seemed as if it would drop off if he simply moved his neck, and the sound of music came out of his mouth drenched in the juice of chewed betel leaves. He was naked except for a piece of cloth round his waist. He was searching, in deep concentration, for the sound that was hidden somewhere deep in his navel pit. The dome of the Shiva temple resounded with the base notes of his music like a tambourine.

As the exercise of music went on like this, in the nooks behind the huge pillars, different kinds of living creatures—like the guilt that can't be hidden—emerged. Creatures whose body parts were all displaced and these creatures that blinked their eyelids over pupils which were like water bubbles waited patiently for the music of Mahaanubhaava to begin. Mahaanubhaava started his aalapa as if he was pleading with a god to grace him affectionately with the song that refused to be grasped by him. When Chandamutta entered the Shiva temple, the hideous-looking creatures settled there raised their eyebrows, half shut their eyelids and looked askance at him. 'I have not stolen anything, so why do they look at me like this,' wondered Chandamutta. Shivering with fear he shrank behind a pillar.

The voice of Mahaanubhaava gradually matured

and began to traverse with ease the familiar paths, creating worlds of bliss. Those who have heard it would know that the new world created by his music emanated from a power centre somewhere beyond the horizon. As the music became intense, the pillars of the Shiva temple began to sound like musical instruments, producing a perfect symphony.

A once desolate world came alive. Chandamutta was all ears, listening to this wonderful music when Mahaanubhaava suddenly stopped singing, and demanded in great anger, 'Whatever has happened to that pillar there? Why is it not joining in the music?'

Mahaanubhaava was referring to the pillar behind which Chandamutta was hiding. The song broke off. The world of Shiva fell silent, and became once again the desolate world that it had been before.

'Some mortal has touched that pillar and desecrated it, master. That is why it remains silent,' someone answered.

'Who is that sinner?'

Once again the bubble-like eyeballs of the creatures looked daggers at Chandamutta. The boy whose eyes were wide open like that of a frightened calf, came out from behind the pillar and stood before Mahaanubhaava with his hands folded. Somehow managing to control his fury, Mahaanubhaava looked at him with eyes burning red as if about to explode. He thundered: 'Who are you?'

'Please show mercy on me, master. I belong to the clan of shepherds. I hail from the milk caste. I'm Chandamutta of the settlement called Shivapura,' the boy said as he bowed down to earth.

'Fie! Fie! You are a butcher who spoiled my year-long efforts at meditation,' Mahaanubhaava spat at him. And as if that was not enough, he eyed Chandamutta with disapproval, then disappeared into the darkness. All the other hideous-looking creatures disappeared with him leaving the Shiva temple deserted but for Chandamutta.

16

THE DESECRATED TUNES

Chandamutta, not brave enough to go in, waited outside the sanctum, thinking that Mahaanubhaava himself would appear from inside the temple. With the blanket on his shoulder and the stick in his hand, Chandamutta was a picture of nervous excitement as he waited, sure one moment that Mahaanubhaava would re-appear, and not sure the next moment whether he was waiting in vain. He resigned himself to what might be an endless wait, nevertheless praying to Shiva to make Mahaanubhaava come soon. The smell of the blanket brought forth a dream in which:

The cattle and the cowherd came running
As if they were chased.
Chandamutta suddenly became a pasture of tender grass
And lay still.
Seven herds of sheep
And seven herds of cattle
Came running.
The red cow Kapila
The branded bull Nandi
The dark buffalo Jakki
The brown dog and the black-white dog,
Came licking the drops of frost

And munching the leaves of grass
Grown over him,
Behind all of them came the mother,
Like the cow which had just delivered her calf,
Muttering curses on Lord Shiva;
And behind her the old Jogti
Like a forest set on fire
Burning and lighting up all around.
And in those flames Chandamutta saw
Mahaanubhaava writhing like an insect
Then Chandamutta suddenly woke up.

As he looked, Mahaanubhaava was really screaming from within the sanctum! 'Help me! O Shiva protect me!' Mahaanubhaava was wailing uncontrollably. His screams were echoed by the thousand pillars and the resounding wails caused the seven upper worlds and the seven lower worlds to tremble. Now the dome was filled with flames instead of darkness. Chandamutta understood that Mahaanubhaava was suffering from some untold misery, and without any hesitation, rushed inside to see what the matter was.

Great flames of fire were soaring
Higher and higher still.
By the side of the idol of Lingam
Mahaanubhaava was lying on his back
Looking helplessly at the sky.
He was in great sorrow, throwing his hands
And legs in every direction.
On his fat belly were
Ugly shapes
And hordes of devils

Engaged in a merciless dance
Yelping and howling like wild beasts!
Their frenzy grew
And as Mahaanubhaava lay burning in flames
They shouted and danced!

Chandamutta then went and sat near Mahaanubhaava and asked, 'Master, tell me what can I do?'

Unable even to look at him, Mahaanubhaava said, 'Sing. If you know how to sing, sing. Quick.'

Chandamutta picked up his flute and began to play the tunes he knew, in his own way. Gradually, the ferocity in the eyes of the dancing devils died down, they looked at each other and blushing at their frenzy, climbed down from the fat belly of Mahaanubhaava and disappeared in the darkness.

Mahaanubhaava was still moaning. He gratefully acknowledged the magic of Chandamutta's flute playing and saw the boy sitting with his hands folded. Mahaanubhaava gently touched the head of Chandamutta and blessed him saying, 'My boy, may you live a hundred years.' He ran his hands lightly over the cheeks of the boy and wiped the beads of perspiration there. He then asked, 'How old are you?'

'Eighteen.'

'Not old enough. Too young, too young. You are yet a babe—a little tender flower. At this tender age, why are you caught in the spell of the song of the old Jogti, child?' he asked, showing his ochre-coloured teeth and the saliva dripping from his mouth. Chandamutta was thrilled at the mention of old Jogti and said, 'Tell me where she lives master, and save me.' As he spoke these words Chandamutta clasped the feet of Mahaanubhaava.

The old man looked at the boy kindly and said, 'You seem to have been stolen out of your childhood just now. Go slow my child. Do you think she is an ordinary thing of this ordinary world, to be reached by mere asking? Even those who meditate for years don't see her, then how can a boy like you find her? It's all right. You have learnt something. Sharpen your talent, grow up. Then, try to get her. If you find her, it's a treasure. If you don't you'll be a beggar—like me.'

'How did you know that I had a vision of the old Jogti, master?'

'The song that you played contained traces of the old Jogti's song. No ordinary man can imitate her song. But your strength isn't enough. Tell me, was her song like this?' and he began to sing. Chandamutta was thrilled. Hands folded and eyes looking down reverentially at Mahaanubhaava's feet he said, 'Yes, Shiva!' 'Or was the song like this?' Mahaanubhaava asked and played the same tune in a different way. 'Yes, Shiva!' Chandamutta said. 'No, it was not like that. See if it was like this,' Mahaanubhaava said and played in yet another way. Chandamutta said, 'Yes, Shiva!' even this time.

'Are all the three songs the songs of the Jogti, child?'

'No. The first one was her song. The next two were your imitations,' he replied.

Hearing these words, Mahaanubhaava felt both happy and jealous. He embraced Chandamutta, patted the boy's head and back, blessed him and said, 'You are right, son.'

'Why did the devils dance over your fat belly, Shiva?'

'It is a long story, son. In my childhood, I learnt some music. Once the old Jogti stormed into one of my concerts and played a song, the same song that you played just now, and made fun of me and disappeared.

From that day on I wanted to see her and learn music from her. I wandered about searching for her. Meanwhile, I received appreciation from kings and scholars. Their praise got to my head and I forgot the old Jogti.

'The praise and fame I received made me vain. Whatever I sang became a tune, whatever I knew I considered that to be the true knowledge of music, and in my arrogance I destroyed and desecrated many a tune. The same tunes, have now turned into devils and roam about on their own. On every new moon day, they dance over my fat belly and torture me.'

'Can you never be free from them, Shiva?'

'Certainly. I will be liberated from this torture only when the tunes are sung in their pure form. These devils will then regain their original form and liberate me.'

'How is it possible to know that you have attained the pure form of a tune?'

'If the form is pure, Bhringi will appear and perform a dance.'

'Who is Bhringi, Shiva?'

'He's the personal and very special disciple of Shiva. His form is entirely made up of bones so you will recognize him when you see him. If he is happy with your singing and dances in joy, the distorted tunes will get back their original shape and I'll be liberated.'

'Oh God! Then I came in the way of your liberation. Please forgive me.'

'No. Now I've understood that by myself I cannot correct the mistakes committed. My liberation is not as important as it is for the tunes to regain their original form. Now that you are with me, we can strive for it together.'

17

OPEN YOUR EYES, O SHIVA

Closing your three eyes
And letting your plaited hair fall
On your eyes and face,
O Shiva in meditation—
Open at least one of your eyes
And see
What is happening
Down below
In the forest of Shivapura.

Mother cow Punyakoti
Having lost her calf
Has given up food, water and sleep.
She is mooing and shedding tears
Like pouring rain.
It is as if
Her heart is being wrenched out.
Oh, the sorrow of the mother:

'Oh my tender calf,
Lines and shape pure and good
Little calf not yet weaned,
Your ears filled with wicked wind
Did you jump directly
Into the mouth of a tiger?

Did you leap over the fence
And fall straight into the whirlpool?'

She asks,
'O Shiva, please return my treasure
And if you don't
I will give up my life
Splitting my tongue into two
And if I die
May no one light
A lamp for you
May no one
Worship you with folded hands.'

She curses
Wails
And weeps.
The skies should melt
The wilderness feel sad
At her sorrow.

Open your eyes
And look
O, Shiva.

18

AVATARA OF KAILASA

Remembering the Truthful Shivalingaswami
We narrate what happened next.
With the vision of Mahaanubhaava
There was a dream of the full moon
In the new-moon darkness of Chandamutta's life.
The hard knot of darkness loosened
The single diamond—the morning star—shone
And the Sun God appeared
Cracking open the eastern hill.
Look, the flood of new light
Has carried away all doubts and questions
The eastern hill has turned to gold
And all the leaves of trees and plants
Of our earth are glittering.

Mahaanubhaava took young Chandamutta to his ashram. The guru and disciple began a new life. With the rains of new light, new water flooded the ponds and lakes. Mahaanubhaava becoming a hundred times greater than a father, passed on all his knowledge to the worthy Chandamutta who, like a true disciple, offered everything he had to his master and received his blessings. The guru taught him a raga for waking up, a raga for sitting up, a raga for standing up, a raga for the sunlight that entered into the ashram, a raga for the light that played over the top of the hill when the moon appeared late in the night, a raga for the heat of the day, a raga for sunrise, a raga for making the crops grow, a raga for the lush green of the fields, a raga for desolation, a raga for sorrow. There was a raga for everything except a raga for full moon brightness, which the guru admitted in a defeated voice, he did not know.

When Chandamutta asked, 'Where can I acquire that raga of moonlight, master?' Mahaanubhaava merely replied, 'Only Bhringisha can tell you,' and fell silent. Months went by and another Maha Shivaratri had arrived. Mahaanubhaava believed that he certainly would attain liberation this time as he now had Chandamutta on his side.

On the eve of Maha Shivaratri, the guru and his disciple woke up at daybreak. Facing east, they remembered Truthful Shivalinga of Savalgi who has the Moon God in his head. They then cleaned the yard of the Shiva temple, washed the floor with fresh cowdung and drew a rangoli. They took a bath in the pond, put clean clothes and tied up their hair. After this they washed the temple with sandal water, prepared sandal paste, brought five kinds of grass, a basketful of *tumbé* flowers and bilva leaves. They then decorated the Lingam with flowers whose fragrance spread to the seven worlds above and the seven worlds below the earth. Following this, they lit the lamp and drew a mandala near the Lingam with black and white powders mixed with sacred vermilion and turmeric. To the left of the mandala they drew the sun and to the right of the mandala the moon. In between the sun and the moon they spread a plantain leaf on which they kept a single betel leaf and five pieces of a single betel nut. Then with the betel nuts, they made the outer form of

Bhringisha in a dance pose, his hands folded over his head. Chandamutta, looking at the green-eyed, three-legged skeleton-like figure asked, 'Whose shape is this, master?'

'Bhringisha's.'

Isn't this the shape that graced me with the horn for my flute, recalled Chandamutta, and the memory thrilled him. He wanted to narrate to his guru the story of how he met Bhringisha, but kept quiet realizing that it was not the proper time to do so. They then drew the divine form of Shiva with his wife Parvati. With yantras, mantras and tantras, they invited all the divinities who came and stood in their respective places. It was night by the time they finished—it was as if Mother Earth had spread her dark hair over her back.

Allowing just enough space for the flames of the lamps, darkness had gathered everywhere. As Mahaanubhaava began to sing, the desecrated ragas gathered in every corner and looked on with anxious eyes at the Lingam, pleading for their release. Chandamutta accompanied Mahaanubhaava on his flute.

They brought out well-tuned sounds of music from the depths of their navel. The temple reverberated with the primal sound of Om. There was a discernible movement in the viscera of the desecrated ragas as the master and the disciple created the structure of each raga, developed that structure gently, filling each detail of that structure skilfully, with its proper soul and life. This act—of giving life to the ragas—which was quite difficult and tedious in the beginning gradually became as natural as breathing, as simple and easy. Both Chandamutta and Mahaanubhaava were in a state of divine trance. The frozen mysteries of darkness decoded themselves, flickered and became bright rays of light. The corrupt ragas were immediately touched to the quick and their inner realities began to assume definite shapes. The pillars of the temple came alive and joined in the symphony.

The shape of Bhringisha in the mandala stirred with life. The eyes burned with bright passion. Life flowed into its skeletal legs and it began to dance! Oh God, the pillars of the temple joined in the dance in great excitement, holding the temple up to the sky! The desecrated ragas regained their original forms and they too danced, mad in their joy! Everyone's eyes shone bright, and it seemed as if a festival of lights was being celebrated in the Shiva temple. Even Shiva and Parvati in the mandala could hardly keep still as they too wanted to join in the dance! Bhringisha's dance of devotion, the dance of excitement by the pillars of the temple, the ragas' dance of exuberance, the music that seemed to come out of the dome of silence, the combined effect of all this made one feel that Kailasa had descended in his avatara on this earth.

Chandamutta opened his eyes and brought the crescendo of the notes to their natural pitch. Bhringisha who had come alive was now going back into the mandala. Chandamutta suddenly held on to Bhringisha's bony legs and said, 'Please grace me, God.' Bhringisha took one look at the boy and was filled with joy.

'Yes, my son,' he said, 'Yes, my son. I liked your music. Ask for anything. I will grant you anything you ask.'

'Then please end the sufferings of my guru and grace him with liberation,' Chandamutta said. Bhringisha was pleased with the boy's devotion to his master.

'Mahaanubhaava, what did you see as you were singing?' Bhringisha asked. Mahaanubhaava threw himself on the earth and replied with humility.

I saw your divine feet dancing
I saw the pillars of the temple dancing
I saw the ragas freed from their curse
And resplendent in their original forms.

'Now you have attained your moksha, go.' Holding up his palm Bhringisha blessed Mahaanubhaava and turned his grace to Chandamutta, 'You didn't play the raga of the full moon. Only the fruitful old Jogti knows it. Go to her. Only when you have a vision of Shiva along with the moon, will you be liberated.' Consoling Chandamutta thus, Bhringisha merged into the mandala.

Having received the fruits of Shivaratri, the guru and his disciple worshipped Shiva with camphor and did a *mangalaarthi*. They then sought the blessings of the happily-smiling ragas that had got back their original shapes.

19

THE BIG BANYAN TREE

The guru and his disciple woke up even before the silver star appeared in the sky. It was still dark. Without breaking the silence around they washed themselves clean, and entered the Shiva temple. Chanting a mantra, Mahaanubhaava chased away any devils that might have gathered in the night. After offering worship to Shiva, Mahaanubhaava waited for an auspicious moment and holding Chandamutta by his hair, made him touch the Lingam with his forehead. Mahaanubhaava whispered the auspicious and secret mantra in his ear and then taught Chandamutta how to draw raga mandalas, how to invite the old Jogti to the mandala and bind her there, and how to peel the layers of her false appearance and see her as she really was. He also taught Chandamutta the mantra for making ragas, also saying, 'But you yourself must learn the secret of making her teach you the raga of moonlight.' Then the wild cock crowed, male birds chirped, female birds beat their wings and a golden light appeared in the east just before dawn.

'These are the signs of Yoga. Now go,' Mahaanubhaava said.

Chandamutta fell at his guru's feet. Feeling the boy's tears fall on his feet, Mahaanubhaava raised him up. The guru's eyes too were filled with tears. Wiping them, he said, 'Go and meet the old Jogti. She will give you victory. I'll worship the Lingam every day with a bilva leaf for Shiva so that he graces you with his kindness. May all your wishes be fulfilled. Just one more thing remains to be said. That old Jogti is no ordinary woman. She can't be possessed by an ordinary man. She can inspire anyone from within but will never allow anyone to discover her real nature. Know this well—she will never accept you without compulsion.'

With these words, the guru embraced Chandamutta and blessed him. Bowing again and again at the feet of his guru, and invoking his forefathers and grandfathers, his mother and the Mother of the hills, Chandamutta began his lonely journey.

He wandered in the wild forest in search of the woman who throbbed in his mind's eye, but had herself disappeared to an unknown world. He searched for her who had stirred his soul. Oblivious to the wilderness, hunger and thirst, to the thorns, wild beasts and insects, he was consumed wholly by a single passion—to find the old Jogti. Climbing up and down hills, he walked leagues and leagues for thirteen days and thirteen nights. The blisters on his feet made it impossible for him to walk any further. He sat down under a big, a very big banyan tree, that was as tall as the hills he had climbed.

As he sat there, he heard the song of the old Jogti floating down from somewhere near the top of the tree. Chandamutta was amazed. Did the old Jogti live there? On the top of the tree? Let me search he said to himself, and began to climb the banyan tree. The tree grew taller and taller as he climbed it—as if it wanted to reach the heavens, in fact it grew almost to the roof of the sky. He climbed for six and three hours, a total of nine, so by the time he finally reached the top, it was evening.

Chandamutta understood that this was an unknown region in the kingdom of clouds. It was a world of light! It was a world without here or there, without anything on this side or that side of the horizon! Forgetting who he was or why he had come there, Chandamutta floated on like a gentle wind in the clouds, against the background of the blue sky.

As many as there are flowers
So many the colours
And as many as there are flower-coloured lights
So many the flower-coloured clouds
Singing lights and clouds
Floating in ragas.

Once again he heard the sweet raga and recalled the old Jogti and his quest for her. There was sound if you sat, sound if you stood, sound if you turned, sound alluring if you walked, sound that lingered near your ears, sound that awakened the body to the pleasure of touch. Oh! This was where all sounds submerged themselves, all sounds manifested, all sounds taken in! Here, in this world of sounds of Nadabrahma the old Jogti must live.

He looked up and he looked down
He looked in front and he looked behind
He looked to his right and he looked to his left
and walked on.

He came to a palace of pearls which had doors of diamonds set in frames of corals. Chandamutta pushed the door but it did not open. He pushed harder, but it still did not open. He invoked his parents and grandparents and vowed to offer them the worship with torches if the door opened, yet the door of diamonds remained shut. He looked around to see if he could find someone to help him. He then called out for help but no one appeared. Finally he invoked the divine foot of Truthful Shiva with Parvati, the Mother of the world and said, 'Oh God! If I am truly the son born in the womb of Sirilakki with the sperm of Machanayka who belonged to the clan of cow in the caste of shepherds, let this door open or else, take away my life,' and stepping a few feet backwards, ran ahead full speed and hit the door with his head. The doors opened at once!

Before him was a curtain of thick black clouds. He peeped in through this curtain—and what did he see? Sitting in the padmasana position on a mat of floral designs, with her hair knotted like snakes, and playing on a flute that was only a bamboo stick, there she was. Who? That old Jogti! If you looked at her hands and feet, she appeared like a bear; if you looked at her face, she seemed like a monkey; and if you looked at her knotted hair it looked like many little serpents. Was she the old Jogti or a female Shiva without the moon? Chandamutta shuddered at these thoughts.

Rainbows and waves of colours moved in circles on her tattered clothes! Those alluring sounds! Did they come from the bamboo stick or from the rainbows? The waves of light became the waves of sound. Light and sound became one. As Chandamutta listened, he felt that someone was playing over him and that the sound came out of him. He was in a trance and asked, 'Did you grace me now, old Jogti? Today, from this moment, my karmas are over. Grant me the art of your music,' and with folded hands he fell at her feet.

The old Jogti raised her head like a serpent's hood.

Her eyes, shining like twin rays of light, seemed to pierce Chandamutta's body like spears. She stared at him for a few moments and suddenly jumped to her feet, seething in anger.

'Who are you? Why did you come here?' she asked angrily.

She hit Chandamutta on face with the stick she was holding. 'Get out from here!' she screamed.

Chandamutta felt as if the earth under his feet had given way. He was not sure if she was serious or, if she was only joking. Or was she being cunning?

'I know you as the night knows the moon. Don't pretend you don't know me, old woman.'

With these words he barred her way.

'Oh you! Born on a new moon day, don't you have eyes? Can't you see? Why do you come in my way?' she shouted, and jumped and stamped her feet, in a mad hurry to leave.

Blocking her way with his outstretched arms, Chandamutta said:

Oh you old Jogti!
Seeming to be something outside
While you are something quite different within.
Your words are marvels, your gestures are marvels.
You have caused ripples in my clear life and escaped.
I beg you. Please don't pretend.
Please don't utter words that cut like thorns.
Don't destroy my happiness.

He pleaded with her in a hundred different ways. The old Jogti rose, the anger of the fourteen worlds erupting inside her.

Oh, you living in delusions!
Who are you? Who am I?
What's this art of music between us?
You utter words that shouldn't be uttered.
Will you leave now? Or should I curse you?

She swung her arms about, wildly gesturing with her mouth and eyes and fingers. Who? That old Jogti!

Chandamutta was at a loss, uncertain about what he should do to tame her. Just then, he remembered the words of his guru who had said that the Jogti would never grace him without compulsion. He took out his flute and played the song that she had played earlier. She gradually calmed down, like a cow in heat cools down, and stood quietly. Chandamutta realized that he was on the right path. With his raga, he created a mandala and a tune to invite her to the centre of that mandala. The old Jogti screamed and was about to run away. Chandamutta held on to her garment but she wriggled out of his grip and Chandamutta was left holding her tattered sari in his hands. He felt great anger surging within him and he pulled her by her hair. A tuft of hair came off into his hands and her old, wrinkled skin cracked and shrank. And from underneath this old, wrinkled skin sprang out a bright light, like the lightning that flashes from amidst the dark clouds! Struck with wonder, Chandamutta started to peel off her skin, and found to his amazement a bright and shining, divine young girl inside. Her body fragrant, her eyes green, and she was the Yakshi called Chakori who stood there, bashfully covering her genitals with her hands!

Their eyes met. Their bodies were aflame.
How should the divine light feel

If a mortal man
Rushes into her solitude suddenly,
And peeled away her pretensions
To bare her naked?
Did the light flicker in this tempest?
Or was the power of otherworldliness defeated?

As the mortal eyes looked at
This blossom of light
There appeared the body
And the body was aflame.
There appeared the mind
And the mind was aflame.
All her body and all her mind
Craved for him and she trembled!

As he saw her
Shafts of lightning flashed through his body
Light burned in his eyes
He perspired
And he was dazed
By the pleasures of sight.

Even before Chandamutta could play the raga to invite her into the mandala and hold her there, she entered the mandala herself and showed him the *amritavalli* creeper that was around her neck. Chandamutta was shocked. That was the garland he had put around the neck of the Yakshi idol in the game of marriage! The flowers were still fresh!

Mara, the god of love, picked up his sugar-cane bow, pulled its bow-string made of bees to his ear, and shot five flower-arrows of love. Then:

Blew the winds of love unsettling the body
Fragrant air filled the surroundings
And she, full of desire, graced him,
The boy who was eager for her breasts and her youth.

She resolved
To first teach him the art of love
She fixed her doe-like looks first on his heart
And then made her way into his mind.

The beauty of her bosom, like a taut bow,
Nipples erect, her whole body thrilled,
She said, I shall make him feel
The taste of the body simmering in the heat of love.

Unable to hold back her extreme desire
She seized Chandamutta in her arms
Fondled him, attacked him
And pressed her round breasts against him.

Like curds mixed with milk
They became one in the embrace
And partook of the pleasures
Of the springs of life, their moans of pleasure
    becoming music.

She pulled him, pushed him, tightened her grip
And her body shivered and perspired
She enjoyed the strength and force of mortal power
And smiled in deep satisfaction.

Thus was tamed the inexperienced cowherd Chandamutta. Chakori gradually descended the peaks of the bliss of union, and wiped the beads of perspiration from Chandamutta's face. Her tender fingers played with his curls and she kissed him with affection. She then taught him the art of music which he willingly learnt. Girijaramana, Shiva, thus ends this section of our story.

20

SHE MADE HIM LEARNED IN THE ARTS

The Yakshi—Chakori—whose speech was music and whose gait was dance, decided that she would teach Chandamutta everything. She made him follow a strict regimen, which was a hundred times more rigorous than what Mahaanubhaava had demanded of him. She taught him all the rules of the ragas and raginis. Smiling, she instructed Chandamutta without even parting her lips to speak. The alluring sounds of music from the dome of the sky, the murmur of bees, the sounds of the tambourine—all arranged themselves like waves and Chakori taught the inner ear of Chandamutta, for a duration of three full moons. She taught him to convert into a song what his inner ear heard and also taught him how to make the song manifest the real. In the next month she taught him how to solicit the subtle ragas, those that had melted in the sky, to appear in the gross world; she taught him their peculiarities and the methods and rules of becoming one with the deities of those ragas. Some of the raga deities appeared of their own accord in his dreams and revealed their mysteries to him. Some other deities inspired him and taught him how to construct their tunes. The moment he put the flute to his lips, all the ragas that he had seen in their hideous forms with Mahaanubhaava on Shivaratri gave him their blessings. Thus Chandamutta learnt one raga after another and became the learned one.

Some days later, in the middle of a full moon night,

the Yakshi chose an auspicious moment and taught him the basics of the raga of moonlight; she then asked him to play it. Chandamutta played it on his flute, but she was not satisfied with his performance. He played again and failed. He tried again and again but each time she said it was not enough.

'What is the sign,' Chandamutta asked, 'that the raga has become complete in all its possibilities?'

She said, 'The deity of the raga will shed its external form and will float in the sky of inner space as pure bliss.'

He asked, 'What do I get to gain, if the deity graces me?'

She said, 'That deity is none else but an image of your own self. You'll know the truth of your own self and that is the bliss for you.'

Chandamutta: Goddess, why don't you show me how to play it?

Chakori: I'm not the master,
I'm obliged to the sound of your flute,
I'm bound to your will.
As fire needs wood
To manifest itself
I need you.

Chandamutta: But you have assumed a form and are sitting before me, is it not so?

Chakori: By your desire
I appear as the Yakshi Chakori
I am but a gross form.
I, in my subtle form, am the Bird Chakori

That lives on the food of moonlight.
I'm the deity of the raga of moonlight
Should my gross form dissolve
I become the Bird again.

Like the artist, Art too is in search
Of the proper.
We searched for each other
I found you
You found me.

Chandamutta was frightened at her words. With folded hands he said:

Is it possible at all to be with you?
I'm just a mortal living on the earth
You're a goddess living in the clouds.
I don't know the rules of your world
You don't know the ways of my world.
My knowledge may not be enough
To relate to you.
Please accept me
With all my ignorance.

Greatly pleased with his innocent devotion, the Yakshi with red lips blessed Chandamutta.

21

THEY BECAME MIRRORS TO EACH OTHER

The Yakshi, Chakori, tested Chandamutta's resolve further by prescribing to him many more difficult tests, and only then made up her mind to teach him the raga of moonlight. On a Monday, which was also a new moon day, she told him to worship Shivalingaswami, a great lover of music. Chandamutta offered a quick puja in the morning and a great puja at noon. As he performed the puja of peace in the evening, the stars began to shine like a million lamps in the sky and soon it was night. Chakori drew a mandala facing the west, and the Truthful God Shivalinga in the middle of it, drew the plaits of little snakes and the tender moon over his head. She then ensured the safety of the mandala with the help of mantras and invoked Bhringisha to protect it. By then it was midnight, a time when even stones melt, and she called upon a thousand disciples of Shiva, and appointed them to keep watch. Then she blessed Chandamutta with the raga of moonlight and warned him:

My dear, I've loved you
And submitted myself to you.
Don't you ever play this raga amiss.
Take good care of this raga

And of my life.
Keep your eyes on the moon in the mandala
And play the raga.

Chandamutta began to play on his flute. The magic of the raga spread all around and reached the star-lamps shining above! 'What did you see in the mandala?' she asked.

I saw Savalgi Shivalinga
Besides, I saw a pond.

Saying, 'That is not enough, that is not enough,' she nudged his left toe with her right toe, embraced him tightly, brought her face near his and fixing him with a stare, asking him to look deep into her. Unable to withstand this sudden attack Chandamutta became restless. Finally he managed to look into her eyes.

Chakori: Tell me, what did you see in my eyes?
Did you see the brightness of my face?
Did you see the light of your song?

Chandamutta: I saw the plaits of Shiva in the mandala
Becoming the western hill,
I saw the thin line of the moon
Rising, breaking the hill top.
Then the thin line of the moon became
As big as a little flower.
The infant moon matured into young moon.
I saw the light of the Moon God
Descending step by step

> Over each and every cloud.
> In that moonlight, I saw,
> Oh! Shiva, Shiva!
> The magic tank of Shivapura below
> And the moon, the cream of light
> above.
> There was a deer grazing
> In the bosom of the moon.
> I saw the dream of the moon
> Floating over the water in the tank.

Then suddenly it happened thus:

From the moon shining in the blue sky
A fawn leapt out.
The shining fawn went
To the tank to quench its thirst.

As the young one put its mouth to the water
Another fawn appeared on the water.
This fawn smelt the unfamiliar one in friendship
Fondled it and played with it, with its antlers, then

The water was disturbed
The waves of light raised their thousand hoods.
The water became still once again, like a mirror
And the two fawns were
Facing each other in extreme anger!

They breathed fire through their nostrils
Pierced each other with burning looks
And waited impatiently to show the strength of their
horns

Eager to fight!
Each fawn grew in the eyes of the other
Like a demon.

How could you say one is great and the other small
In its power and in its cunning? But
The destruction of both was at hand.

It's a different matter
If the desires of both were the same.
But,
One was thirsting for water
And the other for light.

The flaming breath of the fawns
Burned the forest, the still water of the tank.

Suddenly Chandamutta stepped in between
'Oh, moon! Submerged in the water of the tank,
Can't you tell the young ones
That they are
Reflections of one another
And to end their quarrel?'

Eyeing him fiercely the fawn came towards Chandamutta. 'Come boy, climb over me and let us glean the harvest of light,' it said. 'Ride over it,' the voice of the victorious Yakshi directed from somewhere. Chandamutta went near the deer cub and leaped upon it. He felt as if there was a great whirlwind, that the earth was turning furiously like a top, that all the worlds had become one, and that the fawn was ascending to the world of shining light. Now he saw, Oh Savalgi Shiva, that the Yakshi and the deer cub were not two but one and the same. The Yakshi and the deer had become one, and their combined image had become a reflection of his own self and created a path to take him beyond the horizon. They proceeded to cross the limits of the horizon with ease.

They became mirrors to each other
In that vast expanse without any limits.
Both of them contained the other
In that pouring moonlight.

Thus the Yakshi took Chandamutta to the very edge of the silver world of moonlight and then asked him to return. Chandamutta averted his gaze from the Yakshi's star-like eyes.

The Yakshi of the green eyes said:

'Remember friend,
As you float in the silver world,
If there is one wrong note
Harm will befall both of us.'

Her face contained the bliss
And happiness of moonlight.
The bright light of the moon poured from her body
And perspiration from his.

22

RETURN SOON, MY SON

While all this happened in the world above, do you know what happened here, on this earth, which is nothing but a grinding mill of sorrows?

As the promised rains did not appear
The daily life of Shivapura was thrown into disarray.
As the rains in the worlds above missed their tryst
No crop grew in the world below
The plight of the mortal world was nothing less than
hell.

Not finding even a leaf of green grass
The members of the settlement
Have taken their cattle which they fed in the shed
And the sheep which they grazed in the pastures
With them and migrated to places where they can
feed them.
Finding no honey in the forest
Or wild bananas or sweet roots
Or even green leaves of plants to eat
The young have migrated and the old
Have hung on to life, feeding on tender shoots of
bamboo.
With their falcon-like eyes
They look at the skies to find at least a trace of the
clouds

And eagerly await the rains
Pleading with the gods woefully.

In the blue sky
Flaming clouds float
The moon burns and the ashes of the moonlight
Fall on arid forests that gasp.
Birds sweat and boil in the heat
And lose their way.

Please send the rains, O Shiva,
Let our forests become young again.
Let the fresh green spread everywhere.
Let the blossoms fill the land.
Let the forest be filled with
Singing birds, mischievous beasts
And our grazing cattle.

Lakkabbe, the Punyakoti cow, waited eagerly for her son to return. Hoping that he may come at any moment, her eyes were glued to the road. As she pounded the bamboo rice she prayed to all the gods for the safe return of her son. She hummed a sad tune as she pounded and when she had hiccups she thought her son was remembering her. She looked at his playthings—a jute rope, an earthen bull with a mask of flowers, a round jasmine cow the colour of jasmine, wooden goats locked in combat, a little flute, a dancing peacock, a parrot pulling a little cart, and a toy sheep. She had preserved them all and often recalled how her son used to play with these when he was a little child.

Even to this day I've preserved, my child,
Your little playthings.

The small jasmine garden in the backyard,
The well, a tree nearby,
A little parrot in the tree,
A little bamboo flute,
The herd of cattle and sheep that
Listen to the flute,
The wooden tiger that awaits
The calf in the forest, the barking dog . . .

Yesterday
I dusted away the dirt of time
And saw that your garden is as it was.
A calf had strayed from the herd
And as I tried to bring it back
The wooden dog with sharp teeth
Pounced on me, barked at me, bit my chest, O my
son.

The jasmines that you planted are about to blossom.
But there are no rains; someone
Must feed the plants.

A lad like a full moon,
With his face painted white,
Standing by the side of the creeper
Ran to me and hung on to my neck.
'Who are you?' I asked, and he answered,
'I'm your son, Chandamutta.'

There stood the moon,
You had drawn him with chalk,
Unable to set
And in the distance

A comet prowled.
What happens if he rains
Fire over the flowers
And if the hut, house and flute burn to ashes,
And if the people and cattle die,
And your song gets scattered like burnt charcoal . . .

Can I consider all this just child's play?
If so, doesn't the fact
That you are my son and I am your mother
Become just a play too?

That's why I said: someone
Must protect your garden.
That's why you must return, my son,
From wherever you are.

Abbe wept inconsolably, holding the clay toy in her hand. Ever since Chandamutta had gone her life seemed to consist only of the toy which she held in her hand, and the tears which had filled her eyes.

When her son didn't return even after many days, she wept so copiously that she was unable to see even the toy in her hands. She looked for her son with eyes that were like a pair of lamps floating on a palm leaf on water.

Who will look after the devotee,
If hard times come upon her, except you, Shiva?
You who remember only the good things
And forget all things bad,
You who can never be caught in the wide net of oaths
Please send my lad . . .

The God of the clan deserted me,
The God of the house has forgotten me,
At least you, Mother of the hills
Should have taken care of the light of my house . . .

You, Shiva, who rules firm over
The mortal and divine worlds
Don't you at least know where my son is?
If you do, please don't test me any more
But send my son quick . . .

She wept new tears each day. She took vows in the names of all the gods nearby. She did the *urulusèvè*, offered the service of lighted torches, and lighted incense, but all was in vain. She was so anxious to see her son that if she had known the way, she would have even gone to Kailasa and fallen at the feet of Shiva. When her son did not return, she fell into deep thought and suddenly remembered a remedy that was sure to work. Determined to put it into practice, on the next Tuesday, a new moon day, at that time of the night when fiends, devils and demons hover about, she took a bath in cold water, put on wet clothes, took a basketful of fresh cowdung, and a pail of hot water mixed with chilli powder and went to the temple of the Yakshi.

She mixed the cowdung in the water and splashed it on the face of the idol. She laid the idol face down and said:

Oh you pretentious goddess,
You know the hut, you know the settlement,
You look after the forest, you care for our houses,
You know what is beyond and what is beneath the
    sky,

If you don't know where my son has gone
Why should you be good and contented?
Didn't my son worship you?
Didn't he serve you?
Aren't you the one who decides the right and the
wrong?
What have you done to retain our faith?
Why should we worship you at all?
I'll set the limit—
Today is Tuesday.
If my son who has wandered to unknown lands
returns
Before the next Tuesday
I'll make him your slave
And if he doesn't
Your fate will be this.

The old woman poured the remaining dung water on the back of the Yakshi idol, barricaded the door of the temple with sharp thorns and returned to her hut before it was dawn.

23

THE SKY IS AFLAME

As the mother punished the Yakshi in this mortal world, look, the palace of space called the sky was caught in flames!

As we slept happily in the seven-storeyed mansion of clouds in the world above, we felt as if someone had exploded a fireball in our ears. Though we are the Dreams, we felt as if we had seen a nightmare and jumped up startled, like little children. Full of wonder and fear we saw, oh Shiva:

The Yakshi burning like a torch
In the flames of disgrace with the fire of burning hot water
Mixed with cowdung!

She was screaming and
Unable to sit or stand still
The Yakshi was shooting up and down like lightning!

Her face that was cool moonlight was smeared with dirty water mixed with cowdung! Chandamutta stood looking on helplessly! All his strength gone, his mouth dried up and unable even to utter a word, he gesticulated to ask what had happened. Without answering she, like one possessed, moved frenziedly and shouted a warning to Chandamutta, 'Do not come near me.' Her voice seemed to split the sky. Her speech was a river of fire, her look rained fire, and Chandamutta trembled at her bitter words. Perspiring and not knowing what to do, he began to weep and called out to Shiva for help.

We were so used to the pleasant face of Chakori
That now we felt a deep contortion within ourselves

As we looked at her distorted face.
She was the goddess of sound, and
We had never heard her
Screeching thus. We saw
The palace of the banyan tree
Shudder from its very roots.
The Yakshi called Chakori
Screamed in unbearable pain
And her tears flowed endlessly.
She could not touch and yet could not help touching
Her aching body. It seemed as if
She was undergoing the sufferings
Of all the fourteen worlds.

She bit her lips and closed her eyes
Tried to make her delicate and soft body
Hard as a stone,
Hard as a piece of iron,
Hard as a diamond,
And bear the pain.

As if she was arguing with Shiva
About this injustice,

As if she was complaining
About this treachery,
She looked at the sky
And wept.

To tell you the truth
There was no harmony
Between her mind soft as a flower
And her thoughts burning like embers.

How could this Yakshi
Cool and soft as moonlight
Seethe in anger like this?
Have you ever seen boiling moonlight?

Her brows contracted, her eyes burning red
Like the eyes of a ferocious bull—
Oh we must somehow save Chandamutta
From the flames of her anger.

O Shiva do you not see how she is
Wounding her own heart?

She is searching for words from the nether world
To curse someone.
Before she could utter those words,
Before she could give shape to those
Curses that would make the blood freeze,
And shatter the living frames
Please,
Oh please
Console her.

Stop, please stop
O goddess.
Please do not think
What you should not.
If you lose control of your thoughts now
Do not repent later.
If the calf escapes her protection
And comes to you
What can poor Punyakoti do?
What can the calf do
If it is unable to know
The longing of its mother?

You know the ways of the mortal world.
You know what will happen in the future
And you know what has happened in the past.
You should endure and soothe those who suffer.
O goddess, please tame your anger.

Perhaps she was comforted by our words. Perhaps the burning she felt had reduced somewhat. Chakori—the Yakshi—looked at us with kindness. Gradually her anger ebbed. There were no thorns in her looks now. But her brows were still contracted. Several emotions passed over her face like ripples on a pond. And as she turned her face away we felt anxious. We were faced with the gory sight of her burnt back. She said:

This very moment,
Let him get out of here.

Chandamutta, knowing nothing, was looking all

around him. He was truly confused and helpless. His eyes were pleading for mercy. We gestured to him that he should leave and led him noiselessly to the gate.

'Stop,' the Yakshi shouted. The sound seemed to be uttered by a tongue of flame. We knew that her words would be nothing but curses. Not bold enough to ask the reason, we stood still. She said:

What you have seen here, you haven't seen.
What you have heard here, you haven't heard.
You should never ever say
'I have seen this', or 'I have heard this'.
If you disobey
You will die.
Those who listen to your words too will die.
Remember this always.

We were waiting for her to end her speech. When she fell silent, we asked Chandamutta with a light heart to go to the temple of the Yakshi in his settlement.

24

I HAVE SUBMITTED MY SON AT YOUR FEET; GIVE UP YOUR ANGER

After walking for three days and three nights Chandamutta came straight to the temple of the Yakshi at noon on a Tuesday. What did he see there in the temple?

No sign of man anywhere
Not even a crowing crow or a hooting owl.
The rains have remained in the clouds of the upper world.
The crops have burnt to ashes on the earth of this world.

The earth has cracked as the waters have dried up
Forests and settlements have become arid.
The fields look as if
The fires set by someone just now have died out.
Mirages wander about!
Untimely summer seethes
And the whole world seems buried in silence.
The light has gone out
Everything is in decay.
Corpses of creatures
Starting with the ant and ending with the elephant
Are scattered everywhere.

'How will this earth live on?
Has the old God become powerless?'
Those creatures still alive wonder in annoyance and anxiety.

When he peeped in he saw the idol of the Yakshi lying face down. It was drenched in cowdung water. Chandamutta understood what had happened. Feeling that he was made to suffer hell for the mistake of others he slapped himself. Just as he was about to remove the thorns spread at the door he saw someone in the shape of an old monkey sitting there. He went near the shape and saw, O Savalgi Shiva, it was Punyakoti Lakkabbe! It looked as if her tears had dried up completely. Chandamutta couldn't control his grief. 'Abbe,' he screamed and ran to her and embraced her. As soon as he touched her, she suddenly regained her consciousness. Even before she could open her eyes she was in the arms of her son. All her sorrows vanished in an instant. 'O, son! You have come!' she cried and felt all the bliss of the fourteen worlds. She looked at him again and again as if she wanted to confirm that it was really her son. Suddenly, she stood up, pulled him by the hand and said, 'Come, let us go to our hut.' She took a few steps and turned back as if she had remembered something. She came to the temple, stood at the door with folded hands and said, 'Forgive me, mother. I had almost forgotten you.' She touched her head to the ground in respect.

There were not many in the hut to share Lakkabbe's joy. She went to each and every hut of the settlement and spread the news of her son's return. She also spoke about the truthfulness of the Yakshi. She invited one and all for the morrow's ceremony of cleaning the

Yakshi idol. She went to the house of the Hegde, and asked him to come to the temple. She went to the guru's house next, touched his feet, and requested him to come to the temple and conduct the rituals. The guru was lost in the happiness of seeing his disciple once again. Abbe took the guru's hand and placed it on the head of her son and asked him to bless Chandamutta.

The next day, even before the morning star appeared in the sky, Sirilakkabbe and Chandamutta bathed in cold water and dressed themselves in fresh clothes. By the time they gathered all the things that were essential for the ritual it was morning and the sun had come up. The Hegde, the guru of the clan, and all the people of the settlement had gathered at the temple of the Yakshi. The mother and the son swept the yard of the temple, sprinkled it with water and drew a rangoli. Saying that there was no god superior to the Yakshi they praised her profusely. Abbe took the idol on her lap as if it was a baby. She washed it with cold water from the Paatalaganga. She then bathed the idol in oil, butter, pure ghee, and a hundred and one pails of warm water. She rubbed the idol clean with soapnut and soap. She rubbed the back, the face, and the body, hands and legs of the idol and washed the lush hair. After she cleaned the ornaments of the idol, she wiped and dried the Yakshi. She then tied the green Ilkal sari on it and put on a Guledagudda blouse. After thus decorating the idol she placed the golden eyes and silver moustache donated by the Hegde on it. On the forehead of the idol she drew the picture of the crescent moon and put strings of jasmine flowers in the hair. She then lit a little lamp filled with the ghee made from the milk of the cow Kapila. The people blew the conch, beat the drum and sounded the bells. They offered fresh mutton and toddy to the goddess.

Thus worshipping the idol of the Yakshi, the people partook of the offerings and were about to leave when suddenly the guru of the clan screamed. The people were shocked to see the guru shuddering. The people soon understood that the guru was possessed by the Yakshi. The Hegde came forward and with folded hands requested what the goddess wanted. Lakkabbe, Chandamutta and all the people prostrated and requested the goddess to speak out her desire.

I have kept my word.
Hereafter, let the mother-in-law
Keep her promise.

Everyone was afraid. They knew Lakkabbe was the mother-in-law. But they did not know what she had promised to the goddess. Lakkabbe knew what the Yakshi was talking about, and she began to perspire. She grasped her breast and looked up to the sky and down at the earth. Was there no thunderbolt with the god of the sky? If he had one, why did he not send it now? Was there no justice with the gods of the earth? If they were just, why was she not getting justice now? So she thought and beat her forehead.

Is there no one in this damned settlement
Who knows what is just and what is not?
If there is one, let him speak.

Thus said the guru of the clan. His eyes were and wide he was biting his lips in anger. He looked around at the faces of the people who were all frightened. The face of the guru showed the feelings of anger and vengeance and he seemed about to utter a curse. Suddenly the Hegde turned to Lakkabbe.

Hegde: The goddess said you should keep your word.
Tell me, what did you promise the Yakshi?

Abbe: I had said that
If my son returned within a week's time
I would make him the disciple of the Yakshi.
I have given birth to this son
By the blessings of a hundred gods.
I have devoted the whole of my life
To make him such a fine young man.
How can I now submit him as a disciple to the Yakshi?

Hegde: It was you who made that oath.

Abbe: Yes. I know that.

Hegde: Now you must fulfil your words.

Abbe: I am just a human being
My words are often sweet and sour and bitter.
I promised without knowing the consequences.
How can I live if I give away my only son to the Yakshi?
Human beings do make mistakes
Should the gods be so severe?

Please let me know the fines that I should pay.
How can I give away my son?
You know the ways of the world
Please tell me if it is possible to have relations with the gods?

Hegde: Does it mean that we should develop hatred with the gods?
The goddess Yakshi is not a demon of vengeance.
The banyan is her tree and the parrot is her bird.
She is the goddess of the Arts and also Love.
She is always ready to bestow blessings on us.
There are many truths beyond our reach.
The Yakshi will look after them.
You should mind only what happens to our settlement.
Are we happy now? We have had no rains.
Already we are suffering from the curse of the gods.
How can we bear any new wrath of this new goddess?
Listen to what we say.
Do not think of any other excuse.
Fulfil your promise.

When the Hegde was thus scolding Abbe, the guru of the clan shouted:

What? Didn't she agree yet?
I will reduce the settlement to ashes.

He put his hand into his bag. Lakkabbe suddenly fell at the feet of the guru and held on to them with trembling hands. She begged for mercy and said she would fulfil her promise.

O goddess, I agree.
What I said just now was wrong.
Please bear with me.
Please don't utter burning curses.
Here, take my son.
I submit him to you.
Now, give up your anger and be calm.

Abbe said what was to be said and gulped down what she did not want to say. Listening to these words the guru said,

O bliss, bliss!
Exceeding bliss!
Your son will mount the peaks of fame.
Here, take this vermilion.

He then smeared vermilion on the foreheads of the mother and son and asked what else they needed. Abbe was unmindful of everything and sat like one who sit disconsolate in a house that has just been robbed. The Hegde was extremely happy and fell at the feet of the guru and said:

O goddess,
You are our mother.
We have none but you.
Please send us rains
And save us.

He held the feet of the guru firmly. The guru said,

> On the next full moon day
> If the son of my mother-in-law
> Plays the raga of the rains
> The clouds will pour from the sky.

The guru then stood up and threw the vermilion to the winds. At that very moment the sunlight turned golden.

25

I BURN IN THE FLAMES OF LIME

Then Abbe was no more like a human being!
The light in her eyes vanished.
She didn't eat a morsel or sip a drop of water
Or rest her back on the bed.
She was like dry grass thrown into flames
Because of the ways of the Yakshi who gave and yet did not give.
The old woman became a forest consumed by flames.

Having driven away the Dreams,
Young babies with jingling anklets
That occupied the corners of her hut,
Driving them away with her stick,
She suffered like one who dwells in a house that has been burgled.

Like one demented,
She smiled for a second
And then drowned in sorrow the whole day.

'The family lineage is ruined because of me,'
She wailed in front of the ancestors
And beat her womb, for she was the mother.

'Even after testing your resolve
I boldly take your name, mother.
Chant my weaknesses as many times as you like.
Aren't you the one who forgives our million wrongs?
Having submitted my son to you I mourn
Isn't this madness?
You are the Yakshi the whole world needs.

'Chandamutta hasn't a brother
Born before him,
Or a brother or a sister
After him.
I don't have a daughter-in-law
Or grandchildren who come up to my knees.
Tell me mother,
What use is a lineage
That has no one to light the lamp
After the son?
It is an accursed family.
I suffer and pine in these consuming flames of lime.
My eyes know no sleep,
It's the truth I tell upon your name.
Please don't say
I've spoken unreasonably.
Please, O please, return my son
And I will make my family grow.'

Thus prayed Abbe.

26

LET THOSE WHO HAVE PITY, PROTECT

Chandamutta could not understand Abbe's pain and happy about being made a disciple, he led his usual life. What was the use of having everything?

The world without the Yakshi
Is another form of death
And is steeped in silence.

So he said, feeling defeated as he sat in front of the idol of the Yakshi. He hoped that her stone-like heart would melt like butter as he chanted her name in utter submission.

'O Yakshi who walks like an elephant, who can know
your ways?
Don't punish me for the wrongs of Abbe,
Please don't be angry with her either,' he pleaded.

'I can't live half a moment separated from you
Don't push me away in anger.
Why do you doubt me, please give up your anger,
Goddess!
I'll do as my mind directs me, it is an oath in the name
of Shiva.

'These are not merely words
I'm not the one to utter lies even for my life.
If you are not sure believe my words,' he said.

'O respectful one,
O sweet-tongued one,
O lotus-faced one,
O slim-midriffed one,
O complete one!'
He uttered a hundred and eight names in her praise.

When the Yakshi gave no sign of having heard him, he waited for a day or two with his hands over his brows, looking intently and wishing she would forgive him and call him. As the full moon day approached, he became desperate.

Chandamutta felt as if all music had left him ever since he had been banished from the world of the Yakshi. But then, it was impossible even not to sing, he said. He decided that with the names of Shiva and Parvati on his lips, he would sing the raga of rains on the full moon day. The Yakshi had given her word, and it was her responsibility that her words come true; if it rains it is the good fortune of the settlement, if it did not then it is bad for her; it is my dharma that I should do as the grace of Shiva directs me; this much is certain, thought Chandamutta.

The rains should pour from the sky for the song.
The Yakshi of the banyan tree should come here
With love and affection.
If so, this will be the first song,
If not, then this will be the last.

He took a firm oath in the name of Shiva and stood up saying, 'Let those who have pity, protect.'

27

CLEARLY, HE PLAYED WITH TRUTHFULNESS

On the day of the full moon, Chandamutta woke up at cockcrow, and touched the feet of Abbe in reverence; he then threw himself at the feet of the guru of the clan and sought his blessings. The guru blessed him, but he was also assailed with doubts. He himself had no knowledge of the raga of rains and so could not teach it to his disciple. How could Chandamutta play it then, he wondered. With folded hands Chandamutta requested that no one come near the temple till it rained; then he went away.

He cleaned the floor of the temple and sprinkled sandal-scented water. He drew a rangoli and put a pair of clean, washed clothes in front of the Yakshi. Earlier she used to accept new clothes every day, but today she had not and hence the soiled clothes were not thrown out of the temple. He thought it was an inauspicious sign and his heart trembled. He took three rounds of the temple in *uruluseve̊*. Sitting tearfully in front of the idol of the Yakshi, he invoked his father and grandfather, his mother and the cow, and many other gods and brought his flute to his lips. Though he blew his trembling, hot breath into the flute with great effort, what came out was just a whistle.

Chandamutta continued to try but he failed to bring the raaga within his grasp. The breath came out just from his throat and the notes were severed. He thought of putting down the flute and killing himself. But the artist that he was, he decided that his last breath should pass through his flute, and invoking his ancestors and Bhringisha once again, he put the flute to his lips.

Holding back the broken breath he tried to make it whole again, while trying to control the hard breath at the same time. The lotus of his navel appeared to open up and when he tried again, the raga appeared to form smoothly. He made the plea of the primordial root of the earth for the rains of the sky, the alaapa of his song. This alaapa awakened the rain family dwelling in the heavens. He gave expression to the heart-felt prayers of the birds, animals, insects and a thousand other creatures, moving the Rain God and a hundred other gods to pity. In his song he embellished and imitated the gestures of the gods, made them happy and waited for a sign from the Rain God. Then, saluting these gods, he began the mature composition of the raga of rains.

Using the soft-hard nature of the flute to the fullest, he celebrated the glory of the Rain God invoking him by all his hundred and eight divine names. He created the circle of the raga along the horizon and created the throne of the raga in the sky over the temple top. He then requested, 'Show mercy, oh my father'—and then, suddenly,

The rain winds blew
The shrieking winds stormed
The wailing winds gathered
Monsoon clouds covered the sky
Turning the deep blue heaven into a dark, black one.

Someone had come
Lurking
Not very far and yet not very near.
The air around was cool
And the fragrance of the moist earth slowly spread.
He was thrilled by the feeling
Of being in the sublime presence
Of the hitherto unknown form of sound.
He shivered and held his breath back.
Like an artist moving his brush with fear and
devotion
He spread the threads of the notes delicately
And gave a concrete shape to the lingering goddess.
With the boom of the tongueless bell of the skies,
The Rain God appeared!

The size and colour of an elephant, shining with the brightness of the other world; tall, his hands reaching his thighs, lightning in his eyes and smiling happily, the Rain God appeared. The sword of thunderbolt shone in his hands and laughing aloud he said in a booming voice, 'Good, very good, my dear boy! I am pleased with your devotion and your art. Here, take this,' and blessed Chandamutta and vanished. Shiva! The heads of the wild elephant-clouds trumpeted in the sky.

Thunder rumbled
Lightning struck
And rain poured all around.
Thick, dark sheets of water came down in a
Resounding downpour,
Each drop the size of a boulder.
As if the dam of the sky had blown away

The waters merged the earth and the sky.
The song of Chandamutta became
The pearl drops of the rain
Quenching the heat of the earth.

Oh Shiva, what should be our fate, we poor Dreams,
If rain poured down like this as if on invitation?

He made the notes of the flute flow like rivers
And we swam like little fish
Caught in the current, in the swirl of the pool,
Where could we find the bank?

The notes of the flute, like a net,
Try to catch the mysteries of the unknown depths.

The people of the settlement, now drenched in the rain, were waiting in the distance as instructed by the guru of the clan—but as they could no longer contain their joy they ran towards Chandamutta. They lifted him over their heads and shouted and danced. All the people of the settlement—children, men and women, the guru and even the Hegde—were intoxicated with joy, and they leaped and danced, praising Chandamutta.

Lakkabbe, who had somehow contained herself until then, was thrilled by the miracle made possible by her son. She came running to the yard, slipped and shrieked as her ankle twisted and went limping back to her hut, and in her excitement, began talking to herself while waiting for her son to return.

The merry-making went on till three in the morning and when at last the rain stopped, the people took out a procession in honour of Chandamutta and brought him to his hut. They bowed at the feet of old Lakkabbe and went away. Choked with joy, Abbe couldn't even talk. She embraced her son a hundred times and fondled him a hundred times. She put a hundred black dots on his face to ward off the evil eye. Jubilant over her son's success, she then drifted off to sleep.

The hut was wet with rain water and sometime in the middle of the night, Chandamutta lifted the sleeping Abbe and laid her gently on a cot outside. The praises showered on him by the people did not however alleviate his pain—that he had failed to propitiate his Yakshi. Now, when he was alone he shed pearl-like teardrops, thinking,

> I can't live without her
> Forgetting the one extremely beautiful in all the
> worlds.

He sighed. Just then, he heard Kapila the cow, make strange noises in the shed. He rushed out fearing a tiger on the prowl. The clouds had thinned out, the sky was lit by moonlight.

> The incomparable sky-flower
> Had blossomed on the earth
> A unique fragrance spread
> All around the land.

Under the roof of the shed, someone was standing, like the flame of a ghee lamp. His heart beat fast but he controlled himself saying, 'O my heart, feeble as straw, don't tremble so,' and took a step or two forward. He stared in mute amazement—frozen—like a picture drawn on a canvas.

There stood the Yakshi
Under the cover of deep silence
The sharp sword of Love!

When she looked
All that was still began to move.
Her whole body shone
With her own moonlight that spread around her.
Body drenched, face damp,
Wet clothes clinging to her body,
The golden pots of her breasts were
Clearly visible.
Wringing the wet folds of her sari
She straightened her clothes
Thick hair cascaded down her back
And a flower fell from her head.
Rain water dripped from her delicate hair.
Opening her eyes wide
Her face as small as a fist
She stood like a frightened deer.
Vermilion shone on the feet of the lady
And the brilliant moonlight on her face.
Her cheeks red like the petals of lotus
And her lips quivering from the cold
She drew lines on the earth with her toe.

That's what we wanted. We anxiously waited
For the moment when they would forget their
 quarrel
And come together again. We rushed between them
And tried to make them one.
'Open the doors of your heart and invite each other
 in.

Don't stumble on the threshold.
Talk gently, touch softly
And let trust develop deep between you.'

Listening to our sweet words
The Yakshi with frightened eyes,
Eager for the war of love,
Like a cracker ready to explode,
Looked askance at the boy.
Chandamutta shivered,
'Your grace is my life,'
He said and ran to her,
Fell at her feet and washed them
With the tears of happiness and thrill.

Then, Mara, the God of love,
Pulled the string of his sugar cane bow to the ear
And shot his five flower-arrows with all his might.
Then—both of them were lost!

28

THE MIND IS FULL OF THE WOUNDS OF MEMORY

The next morning Abbe still hadn't recovered from the intoxication of her joy. At dawn, she had heard Kapila the cow moan strangely. Someone must have come near the shed, she thought, and wanted to ask her son about it. But he had already gone out, so she engaged herself in daily chores.

Even before her son entered the hut, the wind carrying the fragrance of his youth filled their hut. Like one who has forgotten the ways of the world, like one who had visited the worlds beyond and rolled in the pollen of flowers, he was floating in joy. Confused at the sight of his mother, Chandamutta broke into a sweat. Abbe couldn't fathom the reason for her son's confusion. Noting that the weariness of the previous day still hadn't left his eyes, she asked, 'Did you take a bath, child?' 'Here, I'm going now, mother,' he said, and shaking off his listlessness he picked up his loincloth and rushed out.

The son returned from his bath, smeared the sacred ash on his forehead and offered worship to Shiva, meditated on him and uttered his name a hundred and eight times. Lakkabbe who was lost in admiration for her son's beauty suddenly recalled the Yakshi episode and shuddered. Then, holding Chandamutta's hand, she led him to the kitchen. She mixed some cooked rice with milk, honey and jaggery and fed him with her own hands. It was then that she saw the bruises on his face.

Bruises of love play on his neck and face
Teeth-marks on his chin and lips
Bruises of tender-sharp nails all over his body
Marks of love looks piercing his heart!

Oh mother! His eyes full of the wounds of dreams
His ears filled with the wounds of the moans of love
His heart full of the wounds of bliss!
And his mind full of the wounds of memories!

Has my son been touched by the wicked wind of a woman, she thought. If so, who is that woman who has stolen my son away from me?

The thought of the Yakshi caused her to break into a sweat. That could not be, could it? Anyway, she laid to rest her troubled mind with the thought that she could ask her son about it some other time.

29

HONEY-SWEET FLOWERS EVERYWHERE

Look how the lashing rains have washed away the sicknesses and curses of the earth!

The rivers and brooks overflowing
All rust is washed away.
A cool breeze is playing in the forest expanse
And green has assumed power once again.
We the Dreams who dwelt in the seventh storey of the clouds
Poured down as drops of water and bloomed
As flowers
Adorning the forehead of the hills.

The trees are filled with sweet fruits
And flowers are filled with sweet honey everywhere.
Sampigés burn like lamps upon the trees
Songs drip from the lips of bees.

Butterflies flutter as if
The wild flowers have been given wings and
The sweet-tongued birds that make the trees sing
Are full of songs of bliss.

30

HIS FAME SPREAD LIKE A FRAGRANT BREEZE

While these green miracles were taking place in the forest, the fame of Chandamutta who brought down the rains with the music of his flute spread far and wide, like the virtues of Harishchandra.

The people of the settlement were convinced
That he was incomparable
He became the most loved one
And they praised the fortune of Lakkabbe,
Wondering what worship she might have offered
To beget a son like him
And praised her in glowing terms.

He became the great one of the settlement
The great one of the village
The great one of the land
There was none like him
One word, 'great', was enough,
But people praised him nevertheless in one and
hundred ways.

He tamed the Rain God,
He taught thunder and lightning a lesson,
People showered on him beautiful praises
And named their babies after him.

31

SURYAMUTTA'S FULMINATIONS

How do you tolerate the moon
That grows full every day
That shines brighter with each passing day?

How do you see
The moonlight lighting up the world
And keep quiet?

Burn, burn his face
And don't forget the primordial revenge.

32

HE DESCENDED AS IF INVITED

Mahaanubhaava,
Learning of the fame of Chandamutta
Felt the swirling of the earth and the fall of the Sun God.
When the Master wanted to know
How this great artist played the flute
He sprang up as if he had stepped upon a serpent.
'Right, master, don't you worry. He is my disciple
And if sent for, he'll come running,'
He reassured himself.
Has this cowherd grown so great that he can bring the rains!
He wondered.
He has achieved so much by my grace
Should he not come and tell me
Of his achievements?

The raga of rains is beyond my knowledge, then where did he learn it from?
Did he have a vision of the old Jogti?
This doubt destroyed his peace
And he could not bear it.

If I send for him
He may not come

Thinking that he is the knowledgeable one,
Thinking that he is the wise one,
Thinking that he is the one who brought the rains.
So it is better if I go and bring him.
Pondering thus,
He descended upon the hut of Chandamutta
As if invited.

33

PRIDE IS SHATTERED

We, the Dreams of the whole world, had now settled in the wilderness around Chandamutta's hut. We clung to the fresh green leaves, the blossoming buds, the winds of bees and butterflies, and the minds of hermits, human beings, beasts and birds. We waited eagerly for the moment when Chandamutta would put the flute to his lips. We played like peacocks in the clouds and whenever he played on his flute we spread like the waves of bliss. That evening, when Chandamutta returned with the cows and herded them to the shed, a messenger with a stick came and tapping the floor of the hut with his stick, said, 'Chandu, Chandanna, Chandamutta, the Hegde has ordered you to come immediately.' Thinking that it must be something urgent, Chandamutta ran out without even informing his mother.

Upon reaching the Hegde's house he saw Mahaanubhaava reclining on the cot out on the decorated yard of the house with his hundred and eight titles and the silver staff of authority, and kneading some tobacco! Chandamutta bowed at the feet of his master who lay busy chewing *tambula* and sought his blessings. 'When did you arrive, master?' he asked, touching his master's feet with his forehead again and again. He then gently pressed and massaged the legs of Mahaanubhaava to ease the strain of the long walk. But

Mahaanubhaava merely looked in the direction of the Hegde, his son, the guru of the clan and the people gathered there, feeling immensely pleased that all of them were audience to this display of devotion by Chandamutta. Mahaanubhaava had stirred a fear in all of them by saying that he had come from town, straight from the Master. Now, as if to inform these people of the wilderness that he himself was the guru of their hero, he said, 'Good, very good indeed! You are my only disciple who has succeeded in upholding my pride!' With these words he received the devotion of Chandamutta and blessed him saying,

> Reign supreme in your settlement
> But submit to your guru.

The Hegde, who was waiting for the right moment, now nudged his son, who went and knelt at Mahaanubhaava's feet. 'I'll be grateful if you kindly bless this boy with a little knowledge, master,' he said and Mahaanubhaava consented. Except the Hegde and Chinnamutta, nobody else was happy to see Mahaanubhaava, whose eyes burned like flames of wild fire.

When Chandamutta asked the reason for this sudden visit, Mahaanubhaava avoided the question and they talked of everything else—about the happenings around, about the forest and the town, and about Maha Shivaratri. When their conversation touched upon the old Jogti, Chandamutta, remembering her command, said,

> If you ask further
> And if I tell further
> It will be of ruinous to both you and me, guru.

Falling at the feet of Mahaanubhaava, Chandamutta pleaded to be forgiven for his silence. Sensing the change in Chandamutta's speech, Mahaanubhaava's pride was shattered. But he laughed showing his saffron teeth and said it was all right.

Lakkabbe, hearing that Chandamutta's guru had come, made preparations to receive him. She put out the black blanket, sanctified it with *sesakki*, kept fruits, milk, honey and tender betel leaves ready for him and waited. Her son returned very late. Alone. The guru did not come with him.

34

THE MASTER AND THE DISCIPLE COME FACE TO FACE

The next morning, Chandamutta woke up at cockcrow, bathed, and went to the temple of the Yakshi. He offered sacred food and *bagina* as was the practice, closed the door and stood outside, waiting. The door did not open even though he had waited for a long time. Worried, he opened the door a little, and looked inside. The clean clothes he had kept before the idol remained untouched. Confused, he began to shed tears. 'Is something lacking in my devotion?' he wondered, and fell at the feet of the Yakshi.

He didn't have to wait very long for, like treachery that exposes itself, he heard a trill of laughter. He turned around, looked above and he looked below. There, from behind the idol of the Yakshi emerged Mahaanubhaava, his teeth flashing in a venomous laugh. Chandamutta stood up aghast.

Chandamutta: Were you inside the temple when I closed the door, master?

Mahaanubhaava: Yes.

Chandamutta: Why?

Mahaanubhaava: To see and know your truth.

Chandamutta: Did you see and know?

Mahaanubhaava: Yes, I did see!
I did see the wonder of the cowherd clan!
I did see the light of the tower of fame of the clan!
You are a man of miracles, performing one every day,
By your devotion black has turned white,
I did see in the bright light
The stone idol of the Yakshi turning into a goddess blessing you!

Oh, yes! I did see
The graceful Yakshi smiling
And removing her soiled clothes and putting on fresh ones
And the breeze of the world of the moon blowing here!

Chandamutta: Sarcasm does not become you, master.

Mahaanubhaava: And lies don't suit you either.

Chandamutta: When did I lie?

Mahaanubhaava: Then, why didn't the idol put on the fresh clothes with its own hands?

Chandamutta: I had never bragged that it did.

Mahaanubhaava realized that he had shown himself in poor light. It was Chinnamutta who had told him about the idol wearing fresh clothes. Realizing his mistake but hiding it nevertheless, he said, biting the nail on his little finger of his left hand:

It's all right.
Let's give up this verbal duel.
Tell me about the old Jogti.
How did you conquer her,
How did you get her blessings?
Tell me everything in detail.

Chandamutta: O, guru! O Shiva!
With the oath of my right hand
and the proclamation of faith with my left hand,
I tell you, believe my words.
Don't press me further.
Only that is good for us both.

Mahaanubhaava: Don't harbour illusions of greatness, you the new off-shoot of the cowherd clan! You are tender yet. Wait till you grow up and mature. Is that old Jogti greater than your guru? If you don't want to be known as someone who was false to his guru, tell me the truth instead of garbing it in deception.

Chandamutta: I can't express what my ears have heard and enjoyed, master.

Mahaanubhaava: Then, think things out for yourself. I,

the guru, who is a hundred times greater than the father who gave life to you, mean nothing to you now. And that old Jogti is everything, isn't it so?

Chandamutta: O, guru! You speak without weighing the consequences. It will harm both of us, and the wrong can never be reversed.

Mahaanubhaava: (Like a wrestler who has the opponent in his grip.) Right then. You should offer *dakshina* to your guru, isn't it? To the guru, to the art that the guru had taught you, and all that comes with that art. If you are indeed grateful, offer the details of the old Jogti as *dakshina*.

Chandamutta: You'll have to pay heavily for this.

Mahaanubhaava: So will you if you don't tell me.

Chandamutta: Then, listen.
If I utter the word that shouldn't be
uttered
I who speak
And you who listen
Will both perish.
If I only were to lose my life for having
disclosed the secret
I would have gladly offered my life.
But you too will die with me,
With your tongue pulled out.
Shall I speak?

Mahaanubhaava:I'll die listening to that secret, tell me.

Mahaanubhaava stood waiting for the story, his nostrils dilated, his eyes burning like coal.

'Listen then,' said Chandamutta resignedly. And then he was silent for a while because this silence was necessary. Not that he was afraid of death. But after this he would have to sacrifice his thousand dreams, dreams that were close to his heart.

Achievement is a curse and fame can be another. The desire for fame had given birth to jealousy, which had now entered the heart of Mahaanubhaava. Driven by the desire to make trouble for Chandamutta, Mahaanubhaava had stubbornly pursued him and demanded to know the truth. But we had no inkling that their argument would reach the point where both would be ready to kill themselves.

Chandamutta, ready to sacrifice his dreams, closed his eyes, invoked his father, grandfather, mother, the cow Kapila, the Yakshi called Chakori and the fiery-eyed Lord Shiva who destroys those who are arrogant. He then opened his mouth to narrate but—

The doors of the temple suddenly shut with a thud. Mahaanubhaava gestured to Chandamutta not to speak. The next moment, he slumped to the ground. It was quite some time before he could recover. By then the doors of the temple had opened, and the soiled clothes of the Yakshi had been thrown out. When the two went inside and saw the fresh, clean clothes on the Yakshi, the truth dawned on Mahaanubhaava and he smiled. Without uttering a word, he withdrew to Chandamutta's hut. And while Chandamutta saying, 'You saved me, though it must have been embarrassing for you,' fell at the feet of the Yakshi, there at his hut, something else was taking place.

35

WHAT WERE HER THOUGHTS?

Here, in the hut, Punyakoti Lakkabbe was shocked to hear the news of her son's peculiar behaviour. When her son was not at home, his guru, that same Mahaanubhaava—had visited her and said, 'Your son has befriended the Yakshi. Save him.' She swooned on hearing these words and when she regained consciousness she saw that Mahaanubhaava was not there. She cried profusely as all her new-found happiness burnt to cinders. She looked up and down as if she was submitting her sorrow to the sky and the earth, saying,

> Shiva, you must save us now,
> Please take us in your fold.

In deep sorrow she

> Leaned against the cot
> Decorated with floral designs.
> Her chin on her palms
> She was soon drowned in deep thought.
> What did she think?
> Yes, yes, that's true!
> It hadn't occurred to my foolish mind.
>
> He returns home wandering the whole night
> through

Appearing to have bathed in the bliss of the game of
love
Dreamily he mutters broken words and
Forgets the words as he utters them
He looks, but doesn't see me or talk to me
He comes near me, but neglects me
Like a bee that desires the flower
That is hiding behind the leaves
He is forever lost in thoughts of something else!

Isn't this malaise the result of being in the company
of woman?
Who else could that woman be except the Yakshi?

Not knowing whether I may die this minute, or the
next
I am alive somehow, I don't know how,
Has he at least asked once how I am?
He's obsessed with the thought of the goddess.
I doted on him, a son who has lost his father
But his life has become a garden without a fence!
I can't tell this to the others or ask Shiva about it.

Thinking that only the guru of the clan could now advise her son, she ran to him, saluted him, and said,

How can I tell you, father, my son Chandamutta
Who knows little, and doesn't know much
Acts strange, speaks peculiarly
Why don't you counsel him?

He smiles for a moment, and frowns all day long
Has banished me from his mind, and
His looks tear my very heart.

Every day his gentle face is full of spots
Like those on the moon, and in his eyes
Tired happiness yawns.

'It's said that my son had a physical relationship with the Yakshi. Throw the *kavadè* and tell me what fate awaits us.' With that, Abbe sobbed bitterly.

Listening to the words of the mother, the guru of the clan thought deeply about his disciple, spread the blanket (*kante*) on a square board and brought the *kavadè*. Then facing the hills he meditated upon the Mother of the hills with deep devotion and threw the *kavadè*. On his fingers he added, subtracted, and divided figures and in the end said:

Guru of the clan:	It's true, mother. The Book says it's true, Your son has a physical relationship with the Yakshi.
Lakkabbe:	O, then, what I heard Is indeed true.
Guru of the clan:	But she is not, As you think, the Yakshi of Vengeance.
Lakkabbe:	She is the one who dwells in the sky. How can we hope to befriend or hate the gods?
Guru of the clan:	Have patience, mother. If Chandamutta is son to you, he is disciple to me.

As the Book says, there is many a profit
In this relationship.

Lakkabbe: Whatever you say, she is of a different world.
Her eyes are green and she possesses knowledge that's black and dark.
Who can understand her ways,
Your cleverness may not be enough
To deal with her, say so to my son
And tame him, guru.

Guru of the clan: Many a truth is beyond our measure, mother.
Leave them to Lord Shiva. Anyhow,
You have offered your son as a disciple to the Yakshi
And it's now her responsibility to look after him. Isn't it so?
When you bathed the idol of the Yakshi, didn't she say, in *Karnika*
That you were her mother-in-law?

'Yes, yes, it's true,' Abbe said, drowning in the sea of happiness.

Guru of the clan: From that day his fame began to spread.
Our forests have become fresh and green.
Cattle in our sheds, honey in the forests
Have increased,
Our women are giving birth to more children,

No child is born dead,
Isn't all this enough?
Chandamutta is eager to achieve the
  greatest
When he's still young.
If that's the will of God, let it be so.

Don't, please don't disturb him with
  your sorrows and worries.
You have the Yakshi for your
  daughter-in-law
And for that you should celebrate a
  festival in the name
Of the God of your clan. Go now.

He counselled her thus. The old woman suffered as if she had lost her son again; thereafter she had rare experiences. Sometimes she felt uncommonly happy as if she were in the presence of some nameless happiness of the other world. At night she saw a calm brightness lurking in the hut, but the source of this light she could not locate. She felt that some guest, moving like thin air, had come to her hut with her son. Many a time, the cattle in the shed suddenly pricked up their ears, opened their eyes wide and looked silently and intently without blinking, at her or her son—or was it at someone behind them?

But whatever it was, the Yakshi is not born of blood or bred on fluid. Is she a woman who would live the normal life of human beings? Abbe's jaggery-sweet heart turned bitter as neem at the thought that her family lineage would end here. Her womb, unable to bear all that grief, wailed out the sorrows of seven worlds.

36

WE BURNED FROM HEAD TO TOE

Six or eight moons had passed since Mahaanubhaava, who does not help in our story in the least, had disappeared into oblivion. In the meantime, while Chandamutta was engrossed in the stern austerities of mastering the raga of moonlight, nothing extraordinary happened.

We do not know what kind of a ritual it was. Chandamutta would get up when the stars disappeared and the lotus bloomed, take a bath, tie up his hair and wear his loincloth, drink the morning milk, and enter the woods. We had no clue as to when he would come out. The details of the ritual bored us and we never tried to understand them. We were not interested in entering that dense forest where Chandamutta went every day.

Chandamutta savoured
The love of the Yakshi
The bee was buried
In the fragrant pollen
Of the sweet flower.

We spread sweet gossip; turning the gossip into a playing ball, we tossed it amongst ourselves and played and frolicked in the clouds above the temple of the Yakshi.

But as the notes of his flute fell upon our ears at very

unexpected moments, we stood still, fascinated. Notes never heard before, bits of songs never before imagined swept us to hitherto unscaled heights of bliss. We felt as if someone had touched gently the joys and sorrows of our many previous births.

The words and gestures of Chandamutta had now acquired a rare dignity. Every step taken by him declared such resolution and vigour that he looked like the emperor of the worlds beyond. His eyes, that were like a pair of moons, beheld the cattle beyond the horizon and even the deer of the moon. His ears caught the delicate sounds of the seeds rupturing and of the eyelids of little stars gently touching each other. His whole frame was bright and shining. He played directly to the ears of Lord Shiva who was totally charmed by his music. Chandamutta, even though still young, was involved in a sadhana that was to be the greatest on this earth. Hearing that he was to obtain the fruits of his sadhana on the Tuesday of the full moon, all of us were excited. All artists are dreamers, but no one had cared for us as Chandamutta had, for he held us close to his heart. Some of us collected basketsful of colourful flowers, tossed them to the skies, and enjoyed the feel of the flowers cascading down upon us. Another dream decorated the sky with a rainbow of flowers of five colours that threw up a one and hundred and one rays of light.

Another composed a lyric for the Yakshi and sang it:

Our Yakshi
Who smiles like the moon
And wears the stars in her hair,
Wake up, sweet Chandamutta,
Look—

She has brought Kailasa down
To the forest

Her breasts
Like golden cups
From which she poured
White light—like fresh, frothy milk:

The one who can be made happy with a song!
The one who hides in a sound entwined to
perfection!

And gushes forth like a song
From the haunting, mysterious sound!

So that nothing untoward may befall Chandamutta's penance, a young boy made a clay idol of Ganesha, the lord who overrules obstacles, and prostrated before him. It was then that a great disaster followed. Another boy came up and poured water on the idol to bathe it.

Aiyyayyao! What sin is this! What karma!
The clay idol of Ganesha fell apart—
The limbs and arms fell to one side
The trunk to the other
The young boy who had made the idol
Cried out loudly
A quarrel ensued amongst us
We were boiling with anger from head to toe
We rained words of fire on each other.

That night—
We fought ourselves into Abbe's sleep

And pushed, shoved and beat each other
We denounced each other with angry words
And then throwing a challenge,
Parted company.

So it was
That none of us was ready
For the morning puja of the Yakshi on the full moon
day.

Waking to the chirping of the birds, we were still yawning when to our surprise we saw Lakkabbe, instead of Chandamutta, come to the temple of the Yakshi to conduct the puja. Kapila's calf, Nandini, had also tagged along. This was the first time that Nandini had come so far from home. The temple, the forest and the fragrance of jasmine—all these caused great excitement in the calf, which was running around happily in enthusiastic celebration of the moment. We the Dreams were still recovering from our surprise when the Yakshi, who was wandering about, returned hurriedly, and disappeared into the idol. Lakkabbe could see none of this, but Nandini who had seen it all, shivered in fright and gazed fixedly, her eyes wide open and ears cocked up. For a long time, Nandini remained watching, and then slowly went towards the idol and sniffed at it. Sensing no danger, she began to lick that hand of the Yakshi that was raised in blessing.

By the time Chandamutta hurried to the temple, Lakkabbe having washed the floor and sprinkled water mixed with sandal paste, was drawing a rangoli outside. Seeing Chandamutta come in, Lakkabbe told him to get a garland of jasmine buds ready. She herself went into the temple and lit the divine lamp. She bathed the Yakshi's idol in ghee and oil, and washed it, once with soapnut powder and then with soap before pouring water from the Paatalaganga over her.

Some of us Dreams, in frolic, created an illusion in the eyes of the old lady. So instead of the idol, Abbe saw the Yakshi, her daughter-in-law. Abbe dreamt that she was drying the three-arms' length of Chakori's thick dark hair in the young sun, and then combing it with a golden comb, picking the lice, and tying the hair into a beautiful knot. Abbe then wrapped around the Yakshi the famous Ilakal sari with a hundred flying parrots in the pallu and the Navalgunda blouse with the design of the dancing peacock.

Whatever Lakkabbe's dream may be, we, the Dreams, saw the Yakshi residing in the idol. It was great fun to see the enthusiasm of the old woman and the demure embarrassment of the Yakshi. Beads of perspiration appeared on the Yakshi's forehead at this show of affection even though she was merely a stone idol. Lakkabbe smoothed the Yakshi's curls, arranged them on her forehead, and with her own sari she patted dry the beads of perspiration on the idol's forehead and put *kadigé* to the Yakshi's eyes and a moon mark on her forehead. She inserted the nose stud and applied sandal paste lines on her palms. She then put the gold waist belt and gold necklace on the Yakshi. *Hingara* was placed at the sides of the idol and a jasmine garland was put on her hair. Still Abbe was not satisfied with the adornment, though her joy at seeing the divine beauty of her daughter-in-law rose sky high. She stood still for a long time and wiped away tears of joy, sighed and said,

Oh, my jasmine of the sky
Golden light of the sky

The lotus-faced one
The red-lipped one
Smiling like a bud
Oh, flat-bellied one
With breasts filled like pots
Fragrance filling your whole frame
Who is equal to you, my daughter-in-law?
You have come to us leaving your kin,
Don't you know the ways of men?
How can you want the son and not his mother?
You talk to him, but not to me, why?
There's no one around now
Speak to me now.
Why don't you call me 'mother'?
Don't you like the ways of cowherds?

Listening to these words the Yakshi called Chakori, unable to contain her joy unable to express it, at the same time suffered in silent happiness. She wanted to leap up in joy, call Abbe 'mother' and fondle her. But somehow she controlled herself, uttered the word 'mother' very gently and touched her feet. The old woman's ears heard the utterance, her feet felt the touch of the Yakshi's hands, and in her excitement she moved around the temple like a cow gone wild. Elated, she broke out into a sweat and cracked her knuckles in an attempt to avert the evil eye that she might cast. She wiped the face of her daughter-in-law, stood up, sat down, ran out, and returned with two more flowers for the Yakshi—to tell you the truth we got quite worried about the old woman.

37

OH, THE BRIGHT LIGHT OF THE EARTH

Evening became dusk, as God Suryanarayana
Set in the western hills
The eastern hills opened up and the Moon God
appeared.
It was Shiva's Monday, a full moon day
The holy moonlight
Filled and overflowed the horizon.
At that determined auspicious moment
Chandamutta took a bath
Tied up his hair, and stuck peacock feathers in his
head band.

Clothes not yet dry, he threw a new black blanket
Over his shoulders,
Went to the place of God in his hut,
Invoked his father, grandfather,
And the gods of the region.
He remembered the primordial Shiva
And Mother Parvati
With folded hands he asked them
To protect their servant devotee,
And smeared sacred ash on his forehead.
He then took up his flute and went out.

He took a step forward and turning, looked back,

He took two steps forward and turning, looked back,
He took three steps forward and saying, 'Oh, I had
forgotten,'
Returned and,
Touching the feet of his mother,
Sought her blessings for his success.

Abbe did not know much about the details of the ritual. She had been plagued with bad dreams the whole night. Her right shoulder and right eye twitched. But before she could speak of these bad omens, the words of blessing poured out of her.

May your desires be fulfilled
May you return with success.

She touched her son's forehead in blessing. Her eyes were full of the image of her son walking away. Chandamutta then went to the guru of the clan, threw himself at his feet, washed the feet of the guru, and received the dust of his feet in reverence. As the guru knew the details of the ritual, he put vermilion on Chandamutta's forehead and blessed him saying, 'May you succeed in conquering the riches of the divine worlds!'

Chandamutta came to the temple of the Yakshi and first observed the ritual of pacification, Shanti Puja, went round the temple thrice, and turned to the west to meditate upon the Moon. We kept absolute silence and looked at him intently. He saw us, but by his looks we understood that it was not the proper occasion for us to be there. So we moved away from sight, yet were near enough to hear everything. The moonlight had already ripened and in the dispersed clouds we could discern the shining palaces of pearls, of silver, of glass and diamonds; here and there, little bits of darkness clung to the branches of trees. But as we were seated at a distance we could not see the rituals of Chandamutta and Chakori.

We did not hear anything till midnight. The moonlight that was like the smile of Shiva was so intoxicating that some of us were dropping off to sleep. The woods were immersed in the cool calm of the peace of Shiva. Then,

Began, very gradually, gently,
The mysterious vibrations of the sound
Of Chandamutta's flute.
It was like honey dripping softly
From the beehives.
Had we not listened, so many times in the past,
To the flute of Chandamutta?
But this felt so very different
We were in a kind of trance.
We lost our names, forms and actions,
We fell silent, lost all sense of time,
We were but just ears.

Deep down from inside us, from the very source of
our existence,
The primordial sound emerged
And filled the space, the space became the sound,
Sound was within and sound was without,
'In' and 'out' became one
And some truth that can not be grasped by the
intellect
Was taking shape in that pure sound.

We felt it.
As we listened, we were not our own selves
We felt we had become extremely light
It was as if we had reached other worlds
And were floating in a climate unknown to us.

Space was filled with song
And that which was filled cracked open
And the song now flooded
Like a tank overflowing.

Oh, oh, we thought we had drowned but were
floating! But,
Look! It not we who are floating!
It is the Yakshi called Chakori!
Like a white cloud
She has turned into a white bird before our very eyes
Floating gently! O Shiva of Savalgi!

It is like the lingering brightness
Of the light of the earth
Moving under the moon
Hanging in the eternal blue sky,
Moving like the presence of light mixed with the
source
Of air,
Like love his song has made music
Assume a shape and play itself out through the flute,
Like a kite that plays in the sky linked
With the earth by just a thin thread.

We do not know how long it had been
But suddenly someone filled our ears with molten
lead,

The flute shrieked,
We woke up suddenly.

The flute shrieked
The milk of moonlight soured
It clogged the clouds like dirty mud
The mantra was broken
And the song fell to pieces.
The bird in flight lost the strength of her wings
And unable to push its broken wings, and
Unable to glide,
Shrieked
And began to drop down like a meteor.

As if we were burnt by flames
We cried, 'Shiva! Shiva!'
Thinking that we ourselves were falling down,
We held our bosoms tight in fear,
And scratched our hearts,
We wailed hoping that at least merciful Shiva
Would listen to us and come to our rescue.
The sky that was unable to support the bird
Turned ashen,
The moon became a dead piece of coal,
Moonlight was but a heap of ash.
The woods floating in the intoxication of the song
Suddenly confused by the yells and shrieks
Opened their eyes wide in shock.

Had someone pierced the wings of the bird?
We saw blood dripping.

The beating wings of the bird, its dome of a neck,
Were broken, Shiva O Shiva,
The bird of Chandamutta's soul
The Yakshi called Chakori
Lost her divinity and,
As she fell
She assumed the original shape of the Yakshi
And hit the earth.

38

O SHIVA, DO JUSTICE TO THIS TENDER CREEPER

Invoking with devotion the Five-faced God
With the moon over his head
If you ask us to narrate
The story further:

Someone has dragged to earth
And assaulted the tender, shining
Jasmine creeper in the front yard of the temple.
Someone has injured it, wrenched it,
Look how it has been thrown into a corner.
Those who have eyes should weep
Those who have heart should feel pity.
Oh, God!

The moon who was a witness
Hides behind the clouds.
The birds are frightened,
The air chokes
Day has become night and night, day
Life is in a tumult.

No gods have come to the rescue,
The God of the clan has not been merciful.
O Shiva of Savalgi, at least you

Should look at what has happened here.
Even if a boulder had seen this tender creeper
It would have turned into water,
O Lord, why are you quiet?

We blessed her
May she live like a jasmine creeper in this world
May one be reminded of the full moon,
When her blossoms they see,
And said that that was our limit
And wished the moon to know it too.
Now our blessings and wishes have come to nothing!
Has this tender creeper no place in your memory?
Or having a place, is it not destined to sprout?
Or having sprouted not destined to blossom?

Please do justice to this creeper
And prove
You are, O Shiva!

39

OH! PEACOCK, PEACOCK

In Lakkabbe's dream
The pinnacle of Nandi caught fire.
As if someone had poured fire on it
The peacock's feathers are ablaze
Aré, aré!
From root to tip
There is a peacock at the root of the feather!
The peacock has caught fire
The old woman cried
Oh! Peacock, peacock
And woke up clutching her womb.
Suddenly she stood up, looking in all directions
The whole world was ablaze.
What flames, O Shiva!
The little star is ablaze, the blue of the sky is ablaze!
Even the Dreams are ablaze!

Suddenly she remembered her son and ran
To the guru of the clan.

40

HE CONSOLED ABBE

The guru of the clan was lost in bewilderment when he heard the false note of Chandamutta's flute in the middle of the night, a time when stones would melt. Fearing some disaster, he took some boys with him and went running to the temple, reciting the name of Shiva as he ran. There in the temple, he saw Chandamutta lying unconscious on the floor! He carried him to his house, and as he was preparing some medicine for him, Lakkabbe came there wailing, 'Peacock, O peacock.' The guru consoled her.

41

THIS IS THE LIFE YOU GAVE IN RETURN FOR MY DEVOTION

For six and three days, a total of nine, Chandamutta could not speak at all. Heavy at heart world he stared blankly into nothing and did not, even notice his mother who sat by his side. If her son was hurt she feel his pain? What had happened to her son? The wound in his throat was getting worse day by day. Did some demon wrench her son's neck? Her son could not speak and the guru of the clan would not tell. She cursed that those who had hurt her son may die, their tongues pulled out and cut off. She remembered the Truthful Shiva and prayed,

> Oh Shiva! Please
> Pour some oil to this, my lamp

and wept.

The guru of the clan administered medicine to Chandamutta every day. But no one knew how Chandamutta's throat had been wounded or who had caused—what had happened in the woods on that fateful night.

O Shiva! O Shiva! While we are thus engaged in narrating the story of worthy Chandamutta, how can we say what had happened in the deep woods on that

Monday which was also a full moon day? As you know, we were hiding in the trees, at some distance from the Yakshi so we too do not know the truth. But as we should narrate this story on Shivaratri for a thousand years more we must somehow find out this missing link in the narrative. Unable to decide how to proceed, we were sitting engrossed in thought, remembering Shiva of Savalgi, when we suddenly hit upon a clue!

After nine days and nine nights, Chandamutta regained consciousness and slurred like a baby. Lakkabbe, who was reclining against the wall, suddenly came to life. Her eyes shone but her happiness did not last long. Chandamutta could now only make sounds but had not fully recovered his faculties. He suddenly sprang up, as if he heard someone calling him from a distance. Seeing him tremble as he heard a dog bark, Abbe said:

Son,
It's me, your mother, in front of you.
Why, my dear son, are you behaving as if I am a
 stranger?
Why do you look as if
Someone out of thin air
Is speaking to you?
Who's standing there?
Are you frightened?
Who's there to frighten you?

Am I not by your side?
Why do you start if the dog barks?
Isn't it your dog?
Don't you hear me speak?
Why don't you talk to me?

If you look at me as if I am a stranger
Won't I get frightened?
In which world are you, although you appear to be here?
The sounds of which world do you hear, my son?

Chandamutta gazed at his mother, his eyes welling up with tears and her own sorrow grew as she looked at him. She wiped his tears and put his head on her lap. The moment she touched his feverish body she clutched her womb, feeling as if someone had heaped burning coals there. She complained to Shiva:

This life is your gift in return for my devotion.
It's now melting in tears.
You are the Innocent Shankara,
It's not enough if you sit,
On the burial ground
Your eyes closed.
You bear the burden of fourteen worlds,
But do you find the responsibility of only my son
Too heavy for your shoulders?
Aren't you responsible for the life of your devotees?
Who else will protect us
But you?
Or, are you pleased
To see this young child die?

After this, she slipped into a half sleep. At that moment, the two dolls which were decorations on the legs of the cot came forward and engaged themselves in a conversation.

First doll: Why is it like this, sister?
It's now past nine nights and nine days
And yet the wound in Chandamutta's throat hasn't healed.
Mother is shedding tears,
Wailing and weeping afresh every day.
It pains us to see the suffering
Of the boy delicate and innocent like a flower
And how much more should the mother suffer?
Is there no way out
To end this suffering of Chandamutta?

Second doll: There is a way, sister.
To the left of the temple of the Yakshi
There is a *nérelé* tree.
Under that tree
Is a little toy doll lying on the ground.
In the neck of the doll
Is a needle with black thread.
If any one plucks out the needle
Chandamutta will be cured.

First doll: What's the relation between that doll and Chandamutta, sister?

Second doll: Hush! Look, Lakkabbe is waking up!

The dolls stepped back into the legs of the cot. Thinking that she had heard the dolls in her dream, Lakkabbe woke up hurriedly. The moment she saw the morning star, she ran to the temple of the Yakshi and searched near the *nérelé* tree. She found the doll! There was a flute in the hands of the doll! And a peacock feather in its hair! It wore a loincloth and there was also a black blanket over its shoulder! There was light in its calf-like eyes! And there! There was the needle with a black thread stuck—pierced into its throat!

She understood at once: understood that it was a doll made by some Navatantri Narayana, a doll resembling her son. Someone had practised sorcery to harm her son!

And she, seething in anger, pulled out the needle and threw it away.

42

THEN WAIT, IT IS NOT LIKE THAT

In the hut, the pain in Chandamutta's throat began to ease and the wound began to heal. Gradually Chandamutta recovered.

One day, when Abbe had gone into the woods, the guru of the clan sat alone with Chandamutta examining his pulse. Chandamutta said, 'I must ask you something, guru, in private.'

'Ask now, son. We are alone.'

'Did you listen to my flute on the full moon day, father?'

'Yes, my son. I have never heard greater music.'

Chandamutta suddenly touched the feet of his guru and said, 'It's all because of your blessings father.'

'I don't know if it is by my grace or not. But I'm pleased with your devotion. What was the raga that you played on that day?'

'That was the raga of moonlight. I learnt it after practising certain rituals.'

'If it doesn't cause any harm to your practice and your ritual, tell me, what is it that you will gain ultimately?'

'If I play the raga of moonlight with utter devotion, the Yakshi will grow wings and fly in the skies. That is the ultimate achievement, father.'

'If it is just that, don't you think you are pursuing mean fame?'

'It is a way to know the limits of space, of the sky, father! Floating and gliding in the moonlight, to see Shiva in the mirror of the moon is the ultimate aim, father.'

His heart swelling in joy, the guru embraced Chandamutta and said, 'Good! Very good! May success be yours. Even I felt I was on the threshold of such an experience that night. But something was lacking in your song, wasn't it?'

'Yes, my father. The Om should have blossomed at the right moment. As it was my first attempt, I was playing the flute step by step and knowing what I should know gradually. That very moment someone pierced my throat with a needle ... the music stopped . . .'

'Who was it?'

'Both the hand that did it and the person were invisible, father.'

'How could it happen, son? Didn't you create the magic mandala of the raga when you started the ritual?'

'I did, father.'

'Didn't you invite the protecting deities and establish them in their proper places?'

'I did, father. But I feel that I missed something.'

'It must be so. Someone else wants to possess the secret of the raga of the moonlight that turns the Yakshi into a bird. That somebody entered the magic mandala, made a tantrik doll, stopped your song, made the flying Yakshi fall down and captured her. Here, look at this doll that resembles you.'

He showed Chandamutta the doll that Abbe had given him. Now Chandamutta clearly understood the chain of events but he failed to understand who could be responsible for such an act. Nor was the guru able to help him.

43

THERE IS A WAY OUT

The wound in the throat healed, the pain abated
But the pain of him separation from the Yakshi increased.
He remembered her in a hundred and one ways
He suffered in a hundred and one ways.
The world without the Yakshi was but hell.
He shed tears and
When no one was around
He looked at the deserted temple of the Yakshi.
'What happened, oh God, to my Yakshi?' he wailed
As if his heart would burst.
He wept and beat his head.
The woods had become the graveyard of memories
The moonlight a heap of ash
And the moon a corpse.
He wept
Without feeling hunger or thirst
He wailed, 'Oh, my white bird, where did you fly away?'
He wept.
Why should I live without her
He thought
And left his hut
Without telling Abbe or the guru of the clan.

He walked alone in the woods,
Climbed the boulders,
Trod on sharp stones,
Day and night
He walked, his feet bled from thorns
Twigs and branches bruised his body
He dragged his feet, fell down, got up and
Walked again.
He walked without shelter, or water.
He walked where there were no birds, or animals.

He cried for the Yakshi, he yelled and shouted.
He looked up, looked down,
Looked around and cried,
'Yakshi, Yakshi!'
And he dragged himself on and on.

He was caught between
Two thorn bushes—one big and one small
He first hit one then the other
And fell down, fainting away.
A bird in the bush asked its mother,

'Who is this, mother?
Even the trees and the bushes weep for him
And shed their leaves.
The flowers wither in his sorrow
And drop.
Even the gentle brook seems to weep for him.
Who is he?

'Is he not the noble one who brought the rains
With his flute? We learnt so many songs from him.

How can the song be without him?

'Much as we try to sing, we only weep!
Why are you weeping, mother?'

A cool breeze blew across and Chandamutta opened his eyes a little. Before him was a wretched fiend whose eyes were red; the eyeballs swollen and popping out. It seemed ready to swallow him in one gulp. Absolutely terrified, Chandamutta tried to get up but the wretched fiend fell at his feet and asked, 'Didn't you recognize me, father?' Chandamutta looked at the hairy face half in doubt and half in fear. The wretched fiend lacked a proper form so it was not possible to make out the parts of its body. The huge red eyes, the teeth looking like fangs jutting out of the lips, gave it the appearance of a creature that was perpetually angry. But seeing a piece of woven cloth on its waist Chandamutta gathered courage. Then the wretched fiend spoke, 'Have you forgotten Mahaanubhaava your guru?' Chandamutta recognized him now though he could not believe his eyes. Could this shapeless thing be his guru? As he looked at the fiend in wonder it fell at his feet once again and begged for his mercy. Chandamutta made an attempt to disengage his feet from the sobbing Mahaanubhaava and show his respect by touching his guru's feet, but the fiend prevented him and held his hands. 'What has happened to you, master?' Chandamutta asked Mahaanubhaava who was burning in the flames of repentance.

'I've hurt you by deception. I will tell you the sins I committed if you promise to pardon my wrongs.'

'Tell me, master.'

Then, his every word replete with confession,

Mahaanubhaava said:

As you brought the rains with your flute
Your fame spread far and wide.
But I burnt in the flames of jealousy
As your fame increased.
You had tamed the Rain God,
You had gained the love of Shiva,
Every new story of your success
Drove me to gloom.
My peace was destroyed
Don't ask me how I lived
Bearing those pangs of jealousy.
Unable to be at peace in any single place
At last I came to your hut, to see you.
I was a prisoner of my vengeance.
And then that evil Chinnamutta came to my rescue.

Or, it was I who helped him.
His whole body was rotting with the festering
    wound of vengeance.
He chanted your defects a thousand times.
He painted your virtues black.
He uttered lies and spread the net of deception.
He said he would be my disciple
And Shiva was a witness to his devotion.
Chinnamutta tempted me with a life of luxury.
I knew that I would have to pay a price for all this
In the course of time.
Yet I yielded to his words—
I don't know why.
But renouncing Shiva,
I agreed.

We practised black magic over your cattle.
We tried to make them sick,
We tried to destroy your hut
We tried to render your cowshed empty
But we didn't succeed.

Then we knew,
You had the protection of the Yakshi.
'If you can't steal his song,
Steal the Yakshi
That will wipe out his fame
And brighten yours,' suggested Chinnamutta.
We went to Navatantri Narayana.

That master of black magic
Sacrificed a calf.
And as it died that calf shrieked like a man!
The offerings that we put before Bhairava
Turned black in a moment
And became food for dogs and foxes.
But we would not relent,
We were drowned neck deep in our machinations.

I asked Navatantri Narayana
To make a doll resembling you
And took it to have Malayala magic.

That day, when I saw the Yakshi pleased with your music,
I lost my mind completely.
I did what I shouldn't have done.

Your song stopped. The chirping world happy in sleep

Or in the world of dreams
Suddenly woke up and shrieked.
I caught the Yakshi as she fell
Before she reached the earth
And carried her away.
She fainted then
And has not recovered since.

Listening to these words, Chandamutta felt the anger of the seven worlds surging inside him. But he displayed extraordinary calm and said, 'How can the likes of you do such a mean, wicked thing?'

'I'll suffer any punishment that you give me. But please have mercy on me. To look at the helpless Yakshi is the greatest punishment for me. Though I would like to treat her and look after her, the birds and animals of the wood won't allow me to go near her. With clenched fists the deities of the woods stare angrily at me. All the horrible diseases that afflict men have already taken possession of me. I suffer within as I close my eyes, and the world outside makes me suffer when I open my eyes. No one comes near me as I've become a wretched fiend. Do you think it is a great siddhi to be a wretched fiend in this very life?

'Call me a sinner, call me an evil one, call me shameless, scold me as you wish. That may give some peace to my soul,' Mahaanubhaava said in a feeble voice.

'Where is the Yakshi now, master?' Chandamutta asked.

Invoking Lord Shiva, who is like the gong of the bell, we now release Chakori, the heroine of our narrative, from her imprisonment and we request those who are asleep to please wake up.

This is the story of one
Who filled the emptiness of the world with his songs;
Who made Shiva, sitting in the graveyard,
Dance again in bliss;
Wash away the rust from your ears
Wash your hearts of corrosion
And get ready to listen to the story.
Stir awake your dreams
That may be asleep in some corner of your heart
To listen to our songs.
The very Lord Shivalinga of Savalgi
Is all ears to our narration.
We salute him, and what happened next is this.

Have you ever fought with your shadow?
It is very easy.
Stand near a source of light
And look at the wall.
There! On the wall is your divine shadow!
Now, put both your hands over your ears
And open your mouth. Did you?
There, look at the wretched fiend with fangs and
 horns!
Will he not hit back if you hit,
Jump if you jump,
Leap and dance if you leap and dance?

Do you doubt now?
Who is real? Your self or your shadow?
Whatever it may be
You are the master
Of the darkness on the wall!
Do not be surprised,

Darkness of the new moon
We are the masters of this little darkness!

Have you not seen Mahaanubhaava?
The wretched fiend that has appeared in the mirror?
Now listen to what our hero Chandamutta
Saw in that mirror called moon.

Shiva, Shiva. When Chandamutta fell at the feet of his master and asked Mahaanubhaava, 'Where is the Yakshi now, master?' Mahaanubhaava held the hands of Chandamutta and brought him to a ruined temple in the middle of the forest. Except for the sanctorum, the whole temple lay in ruins. It was absolutely dark inside the temple so Mahaanubhaava simply pointed out the place and did not enter. Chandamutta went in, with faltering steps. In a little while his feet touched the legs of the Yakshi and he said, 'Devi.' The Yakshi called Chakori slowly opened her eyes. Two little lamps came to life in a gentle green light which was soothing to the eyes. What he saw in that light made Chandamutta suffer all the more. With the exception of her eyes, the whole body of the Yakshi had become inert like stone. The snow-white wings were smudged with mud. There was not the slightest movement in her limbs. Her lips were dry and she sighed. She tried to speak, but could not. Just like the oil that drips from the edge of a wick, tears fell from her eyes. Holding himself responsible for her suffering, Chandamutta decided that he would give up his life to save hers. He came out of the temple and saw Mahaanubhaava standing, his head hung in shame and guilt. Chandamutta went to him and asked, 'Is there no way to save the Yakshi, master?'

'There is, my son. But don't compel me to say it. I

have already sinned enough.'

'Whatever it may be, you must say it, master,' Chandamutta pleaded, falling at his feet.

'How can I tell you, my son? I have sinned and even if I offer my life it won't atone for my sins. But she will not live by my life. How can I sacrifice someone else for my wrongs?'

'Whatever it may be, you must say it, master.'

'Then, listen. It is my duty to tell you. On the day of Shivaratri, a great artist must sing or play the raga of moonlight to perfection and Shiva must be pleased with that performance. If Shiva is really pleased, a full moon will appear on the new moon day. When that happens, the Yakshi's divinity will return to her and she will fly in the sky. But where is the one who knows the raga of the moonlight?'

'I know the raga of moonlight. Tell me further, master.'

'Then I must not tell any further saying,' Mahaanubhaava began to run as if he had seen death. Chandamutta chased him, and pressed him in the name of Shiva to complete his words. Mahaanubhaava then pleaded, 'Why do you want me to commit a new sin? I have committed enough already. Please leave me alone.'

But Chandamutta was so insistent that. Mahaanubhaava finally relented.

'When she regains her divinity and flies, the artist who sings the raga of moonlight will turn to stone, my son.'

Happiness shone in the eyes of Chandamutta.

'Is it true, master? How did you know this?'

'It is true, son. I can not lie anymore. I overheard the conversation between her two attendants. I thought I was dead but now I feel I have come to life once again. Please forgive me, son,' Mahaanubhaava said.

'I'm grateful to you, master. If I don't bring the Yakshi back to life, of what use is my life, my name?'

With these words Chandamutta went into the temple. He spread the blanket that was on his shoulder over the floor. He then laid the Yakshi on it and carried her with great care, as if she were a little child, to his hut.

Mahaanubhaava felt relieved of the heavy load on his chest
He went into the temple
To take a handful of the dust from the feet of the Yakshi
And raised it to his forehead.

44

HE WENT RIDING ON THE MIRAGE

Lakkabbe complained to Shiva about her son who had gone away without telling her and who seemed to have lost all direction in life.

I can't tame my son
He is obsessed with the goddess
And the thought of the moon.
If you find him, please ask him to return,

She pleaded with all the gods.

He went riding on the mirage
He went to hunt the moon, who can't be captured.

'I'll capture the moon
Who floats like a silver fish in the moonlight,'
He said.

A child proud like the fluttering flag
Said he would leap to the sky
Loot the riches, seize the sky
And drown us in dreams

'I'll bring the smiles that never fade
From the land of the fairies from beyond the skies,

I'll bring a handful of frolicking twinkling stars,
I'll tame the arrogant moon,'
He said.

He hasn't returned and
My anxious eyes wait.
I want him to return
With at least a flower from the sky
I fear he has lost his way
In the ups and downs of his fantasy.
If you find him
Please ask him to return.

As she sang, she remembered that she could ask the cow for an omen. She went to the cowshed and sat before the cow Kapila.

'If my son who has gone away will return, lift your right leg. Otherwise lift your left leg,' she said.

The cow Kapila lifted her right leg. Abbe felt encouraged.

'If he will come this week, lift your right leg, if not, your left leg,' she said.

The cow Kapila lifted her right leg. Abbe was intoxicated with joy.

'If he will come today itself, lift your right leg, if not, your left leg,' she said.

This time too, the cow raised her right leg. Beside herself with joy, Abbe danced like children do. She fed the calves, gave them water to drink and milked the cows. She swept every corner of the hut clean, sprinkled cowdung water and drew a rangoli in the yard. She churned the curd for butter, melted the butter and with the ghee lit the lamp in front of the God of her family. She then prepared a great many varieties of delicious food. She wiped the beads of perspiration on her forehead and without even sipping a drop of water herself, sat down awaiting her son. The sun set, the sky turned dark, yet her son did not return. But her faith that he would certainly come was unshakeable. As she sat waiting, she gradually fell asleep and started dreaming. In her dream—

Someone came running to the hut
And asked her to open the door.
A stranger came rushing in,
Hurriedly closed the door
And sighed.

His tender face had dried up like a withered flower.
His face was dirty as if he had rolled in mud.
He had tucked in a peacock feather into his knotted hair.
He held broken weapons in his hand.
A sharp star was stuck to his heart, piercing it.
Blood dripped from that wound.
He was full of fear as if someone was following him.
He locked the door
And pleaded with Abbe to save him.
'I'm saved,' he said
As he saw the darkness in the hut.
And he came crawling like a child to Abbe.

'Who is chasing you, child?'
She asked.
'The moon is following me!' he said.
'He is sure to come, he will chase me
In some unknown shape and in some unknown manner

And hunt me.
Save this child of yours, mother,'
He said.

When he said 'mother' her breasts filled
And milk overflowed.
As he saw the milk
'Moonlight,' he cried,
The moon has come
he exclaimed and fainted!

Suddenly Lakkabbe woke up perspiring. She heard someone knocking on the door; picking up a lamp, she scrambled to the door. She opened the door—and there stood her son! He had brought the Yakshi, carrying her on his shoulder. He whispered 'Yakshi' into his mother's ear. She ran to the cot, spread a blanket, fluffed up a pillow, prepared a bed for the Yakshi and helped her son to lay her down. She understood at once that the Yakshi was also a victim of the black magic of Navatantri Narayana. She was shocked at the helplessness of the goddess of the sky. The goddess who blessed men was now a little child begging for the mercy of mortals! The balance of the relations between the gods, the universe and man was lost, she felt, and began to pray silently.

45

I TOLD YOU WHAT I SHOULD TELL, MY SON

Our sole intention in showing the morning dream was to inform old Abbe that her son would return. But without our knowing it, the power of her soul made her enact the terrible age-old truths of humankind, unknown even to us. Was it not Chandamutta who appeared in my dream, Abbe wondered, and not knowing how to handle the situation, she ran to the hearth as if in answer to someone who called her from there. And as if he was waiting for the proper time, Chandamutta came there and said, 'I think you have suffered a lot because I was away from you so long, mother.'

'No. All this time you were a baby in my heart, sucking your little thumb and dreaming about the moon,' she said. Chandamutta gazed at her, not knowing what she meant.

'Mother, I have to tell you something,' Chandamutta said. The old woman was sure that her son would ask her blessings for some dangerous enterprise. She now had to save herself and her son.

I have grown old, son,
And all the marvels of this life are dead for me.
Now, this moment or the next

When summons arrive from Shiva
This game of my life will end
I must then throw away this toy of life and go.
And then, these toys,
This hut, this shed, these cattle, these woods,
The moonlight, and even you will remain here
Scattered.'

Chandamutta was perplexed at the confused look in her eyes and by her words. He said very gently, 'Mother, I'm hungry.'

She brought forth the preparations of the day and fed her son with her own hands.

'Does your Yakshi eat our food, son?'

'No, mother. She lives on moonlight.'

'When will she be relieved of this suffering, son?'

I should play the raga of moonlight on the night of
  Shivaratri.
That raga should entice the moon to appear
And his moonlight should touch the Yakshi.
Then she will regain her divinity and be free.

Does the moon appear on the new moon day of Shivaratri? Abbe wondered confusedly. But since Chandamutta didn't tell her that he would be turned into a lifeless stone when the Yakshi gained her divinity, she didn't suspect any danger in this. Then, she remembered her dream and said,

I told you what I should say, son.
If my words sound irrelevant
Then forget them and go your own way.
I am always with you, supporting you.

46

THAT IS ALL MY DEVOTION, MOTHER

The guru of the clan was apprehensive for he had dreamt of a burning meteor falling on the temple of the Yakshi. He now sat on his black blanket and threw the *kavadé* to divine the future. At that moment Chandamutta came in and bowed in reverence at the feet of the guru. Getting up, the guru put a vermilion mark on his forehead and placing both his hands on Chandamutta's head, blessed him with success. Chandamutta told him of his meeting with Mahaanubhaava; his finding of the Yakshi; of the only way possible by which she would be set free; the details of the ritual and also the inevitability of his turning to stone. He asked the guru to look after his mother and fell at his feet again in supplication. Now the guru clearly understood his dream. He embraced Chandamutta, held him long, his heart thundering like the clouds in the rainy season, and wept. Chandamutta felt the hot tears fall on his head. Gently disengaging himself from the embrace, he looked at the guru of the clan.

The guru asked him, 'Is there no other way to free the Yakshi?'

'No, father. If the Yakshi is not freed there will be no music in this world. If she is freed Abbe will lose her son, the guru his disciple and the settlement Chandamutta.'

'Alas, the fate of man!' the guru of the clan exclaimed, and sat lost in thought.

Chandamutta could not bear to look at the crestfallen face of his guru and went away silently. When the guru looked up, Chandamutta was not there. Looking in the direction Chandamutta had gone, the guru of the clan blessed him.

> Let all the gods of our clan, and the gods of the land
> Protect you.
> Let not the eyes and hands of the wicked
> Touch you.
> Let not Shiva who has the moon in his hair
> Forget you.

The moment Chandamutta left, the guru felt as if his heart had been wrenched out. We, the Dreams, do not like old men, but today we felt sad for him. In the evening, the guru, feeling completely drained of strength in his legs, somehow dragged himself to Lakkabbe's hut.

Lakkabbe didn't give him water to wash his feet with as she always did, nor honey and milk to quench his thirst. 'Does she know already?' the guru wondered. 'If she knows, it is good, for I need not tell her the sad news.' He walked up to the cot where the Yakshi lay and her helplessness saddened him deeply.

As the Yakshi groaned, the old man feared something terrible. 'How she must be suffering, the goddess of music, to groan like this!' he thought. Knowing that he could do nothing to help her, he cursed the fate of man. With trembling hands, he took some vermilion from his bag and put it on the feet of the Yakshi saying, 'This is all I can do, mother,' and went away.

47

MAHA SHIVARATRI

As the morning star appeared we woke up,
The cock crowed, the east turned red,
It was Monday, the day of Shivaratri,

And the Sun God came up.
Abbe turned to the Kailasa on the top of the hill
Slapped her cheeks, and folded her hands in
devotion.
But, tearing away the curtain of her recent
forgetfulness
The boy with a star stuck deep in his heart came to
her mind.
To forget him
She cleaned the floor near the cooking place and
drew a rangoli
Went to the pond for a bath,
Uttering the name of Shiva
She plucked flowers
And put them at the feet of God
In her hut.

Though nobody had said so, the birds, animals, all the creatures, and even the trees and plants knew that today Chandamutta would play on his flute and that the Yakshi would fly in the sky.

Abbe felt that the whole universe was looking at her, and felt feverish within. She muttered broken words, and tearfully cursed Shiva for having stolen her child.

We, the Dreams, felt that we should put her mind at rest by making her forget everything. Do you know why? Because we doubted if she would allow Chandamutta to leave the hut if she knew about the tragedy that awaited him. That is why we showed her sweet dreams to make her forget the child with the star stuck deep in his heart.

Chandamutta hoisting a flag
Atop the temple of the Yakshi,
Chandamutta mounting a stone chariot
Marching towards Kailasa,
Chandamutta sitting upon the deer
That resides in the moon
And wandering about in the world of lights . . .

Her heart pounded within her and the memory of the child, with the star stuck deep in his heart, only became stronger and stronger.

It was her practice to wake her son early in the morning. But as she did not come today, Chandamutta decided to get up and go to the pond for a bath. At that moment, Abbe came there, walking slowly and looking like a wild tree. Without uttering a word, she made her son sit upon the stone seat, took a piece of stone and rubbed his back. Chandamutta thought of saying a few words of solace but feeling a hot tear drop on his back, said, 'Why, mother, you are weeping!' The mother took a long time to say what was worrying her.

'Let it be. I have wept a lot
Yet God has not understood my tears,'
She said and went near the Yakshi.

Chandamutta then offered worship to Shiva and went to the cowshed and let the calves out. But none of them went to the cows for milk instead, they stood around Chandamutta looking at him silently. The cow Kapila shed tears from the corner of her eyes, and stood nuzzling rubbing her neck against his shoulder.

Abbe's heart went out to the Yakshi who lay still. She wiped the Yakshi's face with her sari, and washed her body. With great care she cleaned the matted hair and tied it up in a tidy knot. Then she brought a few jasmines and put them in her hair, and put a dot of vermilion on her forehead. Moved by Abbe's love tears rushed to the Yakshi's eyes and she looked at Abbe with eyes that were like little lamps floating on water. Abbe too wept.

In the meanwhile there was terrible news. Chinnamutta, who had gone in search of the Yakshi had bumped into Mahaanubhaava and demanded to know where the Yakshi was. When Mahaanubhaava refused to disclose the truth, Chinnamutta fell to beating Mahaanubhaava and one's eyes of Mahaanubhaava fell out on the ground. Chinnamutta could not bear to see the sight. He ran away, fell into a chasm and perished. Unable to bear the death of his only son, the Hegde retired to the forest, after requesting the elders to pass on his silver rod of authority to Sirilakki. All this affected the life of the people of the settlement. They were gathered in the house of the Hegde and so could not go to Lakkabbe's house. We too did not break the news to Chandamutta and Abbe, thinking that perhaps the guru of the clan might have told them. But the guru, sensing that it would be most improper to break the news then, remained silent.

48

MAY SUCCESS BE YOURS, MY SON

Life had been an endless tale of suffering for Lakkabbe from the moment Chandamutta had developed an obsession for the Yakshi. She felt empty-handed, empty-lapped and empty-wombed. Thereafter, she felt that all her hopes were dashed to the ground whenever she looked at him.

> Let the song of my son blossom like a flower
> And spread fragrance everywhere.
> I planted a jasmine creeper and tended it, O Shiva,
> But your breeze did not caress it at all.
> The leaves have fallen and the creeper has gone
> dry—

She sang, as she cleaned the ragi or pounded the grains. Of late, she was heard saying,

> My life is a ship without a captain
> Moving any which way the wind blows.
> The ship leaks, and it may not be too long
> Before it sinks.

She burnt out like a flame from the day she had dreamt of the child with the star stuck deep in his heart. For the sake of our story and for her well-being, we showed Abbe Chandamutta instead of the child with the star stuck deep in his heart. Soon, her eyes were unable to see the hut in the haze of tears and she was in a state of forgetfulness. She would say something, and argue with imaginary people around her. We were happy that she had consoled herself.

We immediately saw the result of her forgetfulness. She cleaned the floor once again, sprinkled cowdung water and drew a rangoli. Though she knew that it was the new moon day of Shivaratri, she drew the image of the moon as if it was the full moon day worship of the moon. She depicted the family of stars around him and looked to see if everything was right and in their proper places and then cleaned the kitchen. In front of the place of her family God—the moon, she drew with lime the pictures of creepers, leaves and flowers. Mixing ragi flour with the milk of Kapila, she glued a cake in the shape of the moon on the wall. She then placed a lamp in front of it and bowed before the God.

It was evening by now. Chandamutta tied his hair into a knot, stuck a peacock feather in it, tucked the flute into his waistband and threw the black blanket over on his shoulder. He then invoked his father and grandfather, remembered the God of his family, the God of the clan and Shiva of Savalgi, and came to Abbe for her blessings. As she was in a state of forgetfulness, it was not difficult to get her blessing. When he touched her feet with his head, she embraced him and said:

You are the true shepherd
You have captured,
With your flute,
The hearts of cattle and men
And the green land of the Mother of the hills.
All the creatures of this wood

Know and remember your song.
Now you want to cross the border
And ask the moon
To sow the seeds of song
In the lands of moonlight.

'Catch the moon'—
I throw you up to the sky and wait with my arms
outstretched.
You fall into my arms
I throw you up again
And you fall once more.
The higher you go
The more heavily
You fall back into my arms, into my womb.
Now I'm ready
To fling you to the skies.

Remember son,
I wait for the songs you sow
Wait anxiously and fondly.
I don't know the answer if you ask me why.
I'm yet your mother.

Here are my blessings and the mercy of Lord Shiva.
May let success be yours, my son,
May let everything turn out good for you.

Chandamutta was shocked by these words of blessing. He looked up at his mother and wondered at the primordial light that shone in her eyes which looked like lamps.

He collected the objects of worship, carried the

Yakshi carefully on his shoulders, bowed before the god, and went into the cowshed. The cattle had not sipped water or eaten their grass the whole day. The moment the cow Nandini saw Chandamutta, she ran to him. Her eyes were swollen and red as if she had been weeping secretly. Like the moonlight that flows over, tears dropped from her eyes. Chandamutta requested the jasmine creeper and the cows Ganga and the Gouri to look after his mother. The calves gathered around him and seemed to plead with him not to go. He asked the cow Kapila too to take care of his mother and then started to leave. The lizards on the pillar uttered the odds, the dark dog and the white dog flapped their ears and followed him. Chandamutta was moved to tears, but just then he remembered the Yakshi and walked on determinedly.

As he walked on, there, on the sides of the road stood two old haggard ghosts of vengeance! Their faces smeared thick with mud, noses filled with filth, eyes dried up, their whole body filled with festering wounds, an obnoxious stench issued from them. They were conversing with each other. What did they talk about?

First ghost of vengeance: Look, here he comes.

Second ghost of vengeance: Keep quiet. Don't threaten him.

First ghost of vengeance: He is already frightened. Didn't you see him shedding tears? If the Yakshi was not with him, he would have run away.

Chandamutta was really frightened as they seemed to know the fears that assailed him in the innermost recesses of his mind. 'Who are you?' he asked them.

Both: Ghosts of vengeance.

Chandamutta: Why are you standing here?

Both: Waiting for the sun to set.

Chandamutta: Why?

Both: We want to eat the deer in the moon, as he appears in the eastern hill when the sun sets.

Chandamutta: Today is Shivaratri, a new moon day. Don't you know that the moon will not rise today?

First ghost of vengeance: Don't you know that? If the moon doesn't appear today how are you going to help the Yakshi regain her divinity?

Second ghost of vengeance: Wait! The moon will appear as you play on your flute. Your mother has already gone into labour and she is about to give birth to the moon! Ha, ha . . .

They laughed and then clapping their hands, they ran away.

49

THE GREAT BLISS OF SHIVARATRI

At the temple, Chandamutta laid the Yakshi carefully on the floor, cleaned the yard, sprinkled water, drew a rangoli and plucked flowers for the puja. As he began the worship of peace, daylight got dimmer and soon it was dark. He lit the torch, made mandalas with black and white lime, vermilion and *harisina.* He then drew the skeletal form of Bhringisha and the divine feet of Truthful Shiva at the point where the folded hands of Bhringisha met. In the middle of the mandala, he drew the form of Shiva with ash smeared all over his body, and serpents playing in his tangled hair. However, Chandamutta forgot to draw the moon. He wrote the words of the magic spell, invited a thousand and one ganas for the protection of the Yakshi, whom he put in another mandala. When he finally put the flute to his lips it was almost midnight. All of us began to chant the thousand names of Shiva and to our chanting, Chandamutta commenced the alaapa of his raga, sucking out his breath from somewhere deep down in his belly. The notes were well ripened and hearing them, all the creatures felt life vibrating within them and throbbed with the desire to participate in the worship of Shiva. With the sweet alaapa that Chandamutta created the jasmine creeper bloomed. With his blissful alaapa he made the fragrant breeze blow and made the gods in the mandala happy. The whole world was all ears enjoying the bliss of Shiva.

Chandamutta then played a song celebrating the divine feet of Bhringisha and invited him, the god of the subtle world out to the harsh, real world. Near the mandala, we heard the indivisible sound which suggested the arrival of Bhringisha. Chandamutta received him and established him on the threshold between the subtle world and the crude world, appeased him with worship befitting the gana of Shiva. Chandamutta then commenced playing the raga of moonlight.

Before we could concentrate on his recital, the torch that Chandamutta had lit went out and we were plunged in darkness. All of a sudden, it felt as if the dark Lingam of the ruined temple was reprimanding us. We were afraid as we saw that—

As the raga of the moonlight spread its maya
The darkness of Shivaratri grew,
Enveloping this world and touching the world
Of stars;
We forgot ourselves, forgot where we were,
And felt as if our names, forms and actions had faded
away
The Shiva within all creatures awakened
And was about to know itself,
We were thrilled and possessed.

Though Chandamutta continued to play, we felt that something was nevertheless amiss somewhere since.

The whole world remained as it was!
Nothing happened,
No miracle took place,

Nothing changed anywhere.
Thus our story came to a standstill
We feared a mishap
And did not know what to do next . . .
Suddenly, it all came back.

What Chandamutta was playing was the raga of moonlight which as a rule should be performed on a full moon day. We knew very well that the moon does not appear on the new moon day of Shivaratri. But we had fondly believed that with Chandamutta's raga a miracle might take place—that the moon may appear with its bright moonlight. We expected that light, Truthful God Shiva along with Bhringisha and the other ganas would give us *darshan*, bless the Yakshi with divinity, and shower graces on Chandamutta. But no such miracle occurred. The music of Chandamutta and our story, unable to move ahead, remained suspended. We were confused and uncertain as to what to do next. What did Chandamutta do?

He too was confused and worried but without losing heart he made the Om appear in the structure of his raga. Aware that only Bhringisha could save him now, Chandamutta invoked him.

There, in the hut of Lakkabbe at Shivapura it happened thus:

Bhringisha realized that Chandamutta had forgotten to draw the moon in the hair of Shiva. Determined to save the boy, he stood on the threshold of Lakkabbe's hut, and kicked the door open. It was as if three-crore shafts of lightning of the early monsoons had entered the hut.

What was this noise, what was this ringing of bells! As the cattle in the shed and the old woman Lakkabbe looked up in wonder and fear, the god of the skeletal form, Bhringisha, danced on his three legs to the beat of the odd number of nine. The dark night talked to the tune of the bells which jingled on Bhringisha's anklets—three hundred on the front leg, six hundred on the leg in the back, and a hundred and eight on the leg in the middle! Then, look, thousands of ganas of Shiva appeared in every corner of the hut! They danced and how! Some with their hands folded over their heads, some shrieking aloud, some others beating drums, *talas*, some sounding horns, and they all danced till dust rose from the ground. Intoxicated by the bliss of Shiva, they were wide-eyed, their mouths stretched to their ears in smiles, they danced forgetting themselves! As the sounds of the jingling bells resonated in the hut, and as the cattle stood transfixed, the Moon God appeared and entered the cake that Lakkabbe had made in the morning, with ragi flour and milk! The flour cake god now shone like the moon of the full moon day. Bhringisha ordered his followers to proceed to the temple where the Truthful Shiva resided. The moon cake followed, floating and gliding after Bhringisha with the ganas. The jingling of the bells on Bhringisha's feet, the crude and harsh sounds of trumpets, drums and horns, resounded in the woods. The jubilation of the procession frightened the little stars in the sky and they forgot to twinkle! The people awoke, but frightened by the presence of moonlight on a new moon day, they remained indoors. When the procession reached the temple of the Yakshi, the moon cake entered the mandala and established himself in the hair of Shiva.

The tender moonlight of moon cake
Blossomed like flowers

The ripened moonlight
Spilled like milk from an overflowing jar
The bright moonlight
Overflowed from the pot of the moon.

The tender moonlight of the moon cake vanquished the kingdom of darkness. Invoking Shiva along with the moon, we narrate what happened next. Listen.

Watching the frenzied dance of Bhringisha, Shiva too was tempted to dance. But being unable to follow the steps to the odd beat of Bhringisha's three legs he was forced to be a mute spectator and could only watch in jealousy. However, he understood Chandamutta's plea and his hands were raised in blessing. It was then that divinity descended on the Yakshi. Look.

Her face lit up,
Her eyes shone like lamps.
She arranged her clothes
As if she was going to leave.

Life returned to the once immobile body. She sat up and using her palm as a mirror, looked into it. She then arranged her curls and corrected the vermilion dot on her forehead.

She slowly stood up
She was still weak, she swayed.
She then balanced herself
Spreading her hands.
And as if the song of Chandamutta
Had given her a pair of wings
Her arms spread wide
And like a kite slowly she floated in bliss.

The flood of the moonlight raga filled the space;
Swimming over the ripples and waves of the raga
She captured the moon in her eyes.
Emanating light from within
She, the Yakshi called Chakori, appeared like a
source of light.
As the raga warmed up
She bowed down to the feet of Shiva who had grown
Up to the sky,
And to the feet of Bhringisha with jingling anklets,
She invoked the ganas of Shiva,
Looked at Chandamutta
From the corner of her eyes,
Her looks full of love and pride,
She beat her wings,
In rhythm to the beat of his song
Swimming in tender moonlight
She soared higher and higher . . .

Playing on his flute, Chandamutta was in a trance-like state. He looked at the divine feet of Shiva who had the moon in his head:

He saw a pond at the feet of Shiva,
And a lotus with three petals in that pond!
And in the lotus he saw
Shiva in meditation,
Standing upon a platform of flames!
He saw Shiva transforming and becoming all the
worlds!
His feet filled the whole earth
And his head that held the moon cake.
Oh that bright face

Filled the space beyond the world of light!
And in between Chandamutta saw
Gods, demons, ghosts,
Fiends, ants and eighty hundred thousand creatures
Dwelling in the form of Shiva!
The Great One,
The Deep One,
The Subtle One,
I bow down to you
Shiva of Savalgi,
I am blessed.

Chandamutta felt his legs turning cold and he understood that he was turning to stone. With great effort, he attempted to complete the raga he was playing. The Yakshi in flight realized this, and her heart ached. 'Oh my dear Chandamutta!' she shrieked and her radiant face turned dark. She looked at the divine feet of Shiva in fear and entreaty. She wished she could die so that Chandamutta could live. In sheer helplessness, she beat her heart and prayed.

Shiva, Shiva,
You who answers the call of faith,
You the conqueror of Markandeya
Open your fiery eyes
And look at the stone that swallows Chandamutta.

Help, O Shiva,
Help our truth, our love
Help our devotion.

Oh merciful Bhringisha,

Save Chandamutta from this stone.
He is giving up his life
For me, for the world;
Save him, Oh! Save him.
Is there no thunderbolt with the Sky God?
Is there no justice among the gods gathered here?
Oh! Shiva, make me stone too.

She pleaded and even asked us, the Dreams, to plead for her. 'You are taking away my life, my love,' she accused us. Unable to swim against the flood of her tears, we stood still. She descended and saw that the whole body of Chandamutta, barring his face had already turned to stone.

She looked deep into his eyes.
What was there?
The eye was a mirror
And in that mirror was
The space that looked upon itself.

We stood in deep sorrow. In gratefulness, or was it because it was to be for the last time, the Yakshi kissed the lips of Chandamutta for a long, long time. To tell you the truth, even Shiva who dwells in the graveyard, felt a tear or two in his eyes, but even he was helpless. Chandamutta's lips too then turned to stone and the Yakshi moved away reluctantly. But there was a look of contentment on her face, as if she had sucked his soul into herself. She flew up, the sky her destination. As she flew up, the Yakshi became the bird Chakori, and she flew towards the moon in the head of Shiva, the land of bliss. Only the moon shone brightly over Chakori.

She reached the moon and looked into the moon
mirror.
The moon himself was flying,
Swimming in his own light.
Chakori swallowed the moon.

Chakori and the moon became one
And there was just one space.
It was a new morning then.

The world of Shiva that Chandamutta had created with his music disappeared into the mandala. The moon cake had turned to ash.

Everything was over. But under the jasmine creeper, we saw a bear nodding in sleep. Silver hair on its head, a toothless mouth, hands and feet that looked like thin sticks, eyes sunk deep, skin hanging loose, she sat there, like a tree twisted up after a great flood. Who was she? It was Lakkabbe! She was still in a stupor, and we wished her to remain so, so that she remained unaware of the fect that her son had turned to stone. We were in a hurry to complete our tale, so one of us asked her—

Mother, mother,
You hid a little bird,
Your bird,
Of the little feet, little beak,
Bright colour,
Tongue sweet
As honey.
Where is that bird now?
It played on our palms,
Sang the songs of the worlds without shadows,
The bird rare to find in all the three worlds,

Where is its song now?

To this Abbe answered—

Yes my son,
My bosom and my womb
Were not fortunate enough
To have it.

Today
It demanded milk for its hunger.
'How can I find milk in my dried up breast, son?' I said.

'I'll drink the milk
That's in the moon pot,
I'll know the limits of the sky
Which they say should not be known,'
Said the bird
And flew away.

My body still feels the weight of the bird.
Now it will sing a lullaby
To make me sleep.

Have you ever heard
Of a child singing a lullaby
To its mother?

Sleep, sleep
Sleep my white bird, sleep . . .
I made the moon a mirror
And kept it in front of you.
The image merged with the reflection

The space has become spaceless
Sleep my child, sleep,
Sleep my light, sleep . . .

she said. Unable to bear the sorrow of the mother, we wept. We prayed that she remain in her state of forgetfulness.

The whole body of Chandamutta is turned
To stone
He is now a stone among stones.
But his eyes look like beads of glass
And in those eyes we find the frozen moon.
But the tears that had gathered in his eyes
Have remained tears.

The saint of light!
Do not say that Chandamutta is dead.
Give the song on his lips to the birds.
Pour the tears on his eyes to the trees and plants.

Fill your souls
With the moonlight of Chandamutta
And carry it with you.

The cock crows
Giving the assurance of warm light.
There is the ash of the moon cake in the mandala.
Put that sacred ash on your foreheads.

Here we end our story,
Here we conclude.
Bless us, O Shiva.

GLOSSARY

Abbe - mother; a respectful way of addressing an older woman.

Amritavalli - a creeper supposed to have medicinal qualities and the capacity to give long life.

Bilva - a bael leaf believed to be dear to Lord Shiva.

Bagina - a present offered to a goddess and/or a married woman.

Chandike - a stringed musical instrument that is played to the accompaniment of songs, sung in praise of Goddess Chandeshwari.

Chinnikolu - a game, where a wooden piece is placed on the ground and another wooden piece is employed to hit it into the air.

Halaba - an old man; he often does the work of a messenger.

Harisina - turmeric.

Hingara - the tender blossom of coconut.

Jogti - a female yogi.

Kadigé - a blackish-coloured cosmetic applied to the eyes.

Kavadé - a kind of dice.

Mandala - a circle.

Markandeya - a young devotee who was fated to die in his sixteenth year but was saved by Shiva.

Mudde - food prepared with ragi.

Navatantri Narayana - sorcerer Narayana

Nadabrahma - Brahma, the god of sound.
Nérelé - a tree with purple berries.
Ragi - a kind of grain much cultivated in South India.
Sampigé - champak.
Sesakki - rice.
Tambula - betel leaf and betel nut.
Tapas - penance.
Tumbé - a very common little white flower.
Urulusévé - a religious penance which consists in rolling the body to the right for a considerable distance, or round a temple.

PENGUIN BOOKS
CHAKORI

Chandrasekhar Kambar was born in 1937. He is one of the leading Kannada writers of our time, equally well known as a poet, playwright and novelist. His best-known plays are *Jokumaraswamy* and *Sirisampigé*; collections of his poems include *Takarainavaru* and *Savirada Neralu*. He has also edited collections of folk songs, folktales and folk plays, two studies on folk theatre and a folklore dictionary. He is also a film director and academician.

In 1991, Kambar won the Sahitya Akademi award. His other honours include the Karnataka Sahitya Akademi award and the Vardhaman Prashasti and Kamaladevi Chattopadhyaya awards.

Chandrasekhar Kambar lives in Bangalore.

*

O. L. Nagabhushana Swamy is an eminent Kannada prose author and translator, and also a leading critic of Kannada literature. He has to his credit several publications and awards including the Karnataka Sahitya Akademi award. Earlier a professor in the Department of Translation in Kannada University, Hampi, he now teaches at Maharani's Arts College, Bangalore.

*

Pranava Manjari is a Kannada critic and translator. She has taught English for five years in Jyoti Nivas College, Bangalore. Now based in Delhi, she writes book reviews for *Indian Literature.*

*

H.S. Shiva Prakash is a reputed modern Kannada poet, playwright and translator. He won the Sangeet Natak Akademi award in 1997 for best playwright. His other honours include the Karnataka Sahitya Akademi and Natak awards. He is the editor of *Indian Literature*, the Sahitya Akademi's bi-monthly journal.